BTEC Level 3 National Study Skills Guide in Performing Arts

Welcome to your Study Skills Guide! You can make it your own – start by adding your personal and course details below...

Learner's name: ______________________

BTEC course title: ______________________

Date started: ______________________

Mandatory units:

____

____

____

Optional units:

____

____

____

____

Centre name: ______________________

Centre address:

____

____

____

Tutor's name: ______________________

Published by Pearson Education Limited, a company incorporated in England and Wales, having its registered office at Edinburgh Gate, Harlow, Essex, CM20 2JE. Registered company number: 872828

Edexcel is a registered trademark of Edexcel Limited

First published 2010

13 12 11

10 9 8 7 6 5 4

British Library Cataloguing in Publication Data

A catalogue record for this book is available from the British Library

ISBN 978 1 84690 566 7

Typeset and edited by Sparks Publishing Services Ltd
Cover design by Visual Philosophy by eMC Design
Cover photo/illustration © Press Association Images/AP/Vadim Ghirda
Printed in Scotland by Scotprint

Acknowledgements
The author and publisher would like to thank the following individuals and organisations for permission to reproduce photographs:

Alamy Images: Angela Hampton Picture Library 19, Claudia Wiens 56; **Corbis:** 66; **iStockphoto:** Chris Schmidt 33; **Pearson Education Ltd:** Steve Shott 28, Ian Wedgewood 49; **Pearson Education Ltd:** Ken Wilson-Max 9, 10, 74

Cover images: *Front:* **Press Association:** VADIM GHIRDA / AP

All other images © Pearson Education

Every effort has been made to contact copyright holders of material reproduced in this book. Any omissions will be rectified in subsequent printings if notice is given to the publishers.

Websites
Go to www.pearsonhotlinks.co.uk to gain access to the relevant website links and information on how they can aid your studies. When you access the site, search for either the title BTEC Level 3 National Study Skills Guide in Performing Arts or ISBN 9781846905667.

Contents

Introduction: Ten steps to success in your BTEC Level 3 National 5

Step One: Understand your course and how it works 9

Step Two: Understand how you are assessed and graded 17

Step Three: Understand yourself 21

Step Four: Use your time wisely 25

Step Five: Utilise all your resources 31

Step Six: Understand your assessment 35

Step Seven: Work productively as a member of a group 47

Step Eight: Understand how to research and analyse information 53

Step Nine: Make an effective presentation 65

Step Ten: Maximise your opportunities and manage your problems 71

Skills building 75

Answers 85

Useful terms 87

Popular progression pathways

General qualification	Vocationally related qualification	Applied qualification
Undergraduate Degree	BTEC Higher National	Foundation Degree
GCE AS and A level	BTEC National	Advanced Diploma

Ten steps to success in your BTEC Level 3 National

This Study Skills Guide has been written to help you achieve the best result possible on your BTEC Level 3 National course. At the start of a new course you may feel both quite excited but also a little apprehensive. Taking a BTEC Level 3 National qualification has many benefits and is a major stepping stone towards your future career. Using this Study Skills Guide will help you get the most out of your course from the start.

During **induction** sessions at the start of your course, your tutor will explain important information, but it can be difficult to remember everything and that's when you'll find this Study Skills Guide invaluable. Look at it whenever you want to check anything related to your course. It provides all the essential facts you need and has a Useful terms section to explain specialist terms, words and phrases, including some that you will see highlighted in this book in bold type.

TOP TIP

Use this Study Skills Guide at your own pace. Dip in to find what you need. Look back at it whenever you have a problem or query.

This Study Skills Guide covers the skills you'll need to do well in your course – such as managing your time, researching and analysing information and preparing a presentation.

- Use the **Top tips** to make your life easier as you go.
- Use the **Key points** to help you to stay focused on the essentials.
- Use the **Action points** to check what you need to know or do now.
- Use the **Case studies** to relate information to your chosen sector and vocational area.
- Use the **Activities** to test your knowledge and skills.
- Use the **Useful terms** section to check the meaning of specialist terms.

This Study Skills Guide has been designed to work alongside the Edexcel Student Book for BTEC Level 3 National Performing Arts (Edexcel, 2010). This Student Book includes the main knowledge you'll need, with tips from BTEC experts, Edexcel assignment tips, assessment activities and up-to-date case studies from industry experts, plus handy references to your Study Skills Guide.

This Study Skills Guide is divided into ten steps, each relating to a key aspect of your studies, from understanding assessment to time management to maximising opportunities. Concentrate on getting things right one step at a time. Thousands of learners have achieved BTEC Level 3 National qualifications and are now studying for a degree, or building a successful career at work. Using this Study Skills Guide, and believing in your own abilities, will help you achieve your future goals, too.

Introduction to the Performing Arts sector

Choosing to study a BTEC National in Performing Arts is an excellent decision to make for lots of different reasons.

For many of you this will be an important step on the road to a career in an industry that employs a huge number of people who undertake a wide range of job roles using an array of different skills and techniques.

The Performing Arts Pathways

In order to cover the skills and techniques for the many possible career paths in the performing arts industry the BTEC National in Performing Arts is available in a number of different pathways.

- **Acting**
  If you are completing this pathway you will study of a range of units that will allow you to develop and improve skills and techniques used by actors. You will work on your vocal and movement skills, as well as your ability to explore and take on characters in a range of performance projects. You may also have the opportunity to study specialist units such as Directing, Script Writing, Film & TV Acting and Stand-Up Comic Technique.
- **Dance**
  The dance pathway will allow you to develop and improve your movement and interpretive skills. The programme will allow you to take part in performances in a range of different dance styles such as Jazz, Urban, Ballet, Tap and Contemporary. Your programme may also provide you with the opportunity to study choreographic skills as well as specialist units such as Musical Theatre, Circus Acrobatics and Mime.
- **Musical Theatre**
  If you have chosen a programme in musical theatre you will study the three key performance areas of acting, music and dance. As well as developing these skills through a range of performance projects, you may also have the opportunity to study specialist units such as Singing Skills for Actors and Dancers, Theatre for Children and Variety Performance.
- **Physical Theatre**
  Physical theatre is a hybrid performance type that combines acting and dance skills. If you are studying this programme you will work to develop your acting and dance skills through a range of performance projects. You may also have the opportunity to study specialist units such as Site Specific Performance, Performing with Masks and Developing Styles in Clowning.
- **General Pathway**
  This general pathway allows you to gain more general experience of the techniques required for stage performance. If you have opted for this unit your programme may include a mixture of acting, dance and musical theatre units.

Why did you select the pathway you did?

In the space below answer the questions about your choice.

My pathway:
What were your main reasons for choosing this pathway?
What kinds of job roles might your pathway lead to?

What kinds of activities will you be undertaking during your time on the course?
What are you most looking forward to on your particular BTEC pathway?

Skills for your sector

Depending on the pathway you are studying and the specialist units you are covering, you will develop a range of performance skills while you are completing your BTEC National in Performing Arts.

Performance-related skills

- **Vocal skills as an actor**
  The voice is one of the actor's most important tools and this programme will help you to learn how your voice works, how to use it as a performer and how to look after it to avoid problems caused by overuse or misuse.
- **Movement skills as an actor**
  When you act you need to embody the character you play by moving as the character would. To do this you must learn to have control of your movements by developing strength, flexibility and self-awareness.
- **Developing a character**
  The ability to develop realistic and believable characters is a core skill that every actor must possess. Your BTEC will allow you to develop and improve character development techniques through a range of group and individual activities.
- **Performing in role**
  Your course will provide you with a range of opportunities to develop and improve your performance skills. Some of the performances you take part in may be low-key classroom presentations, while others may be full-scale theatrical events. Either way you will need to develop performance skills to enable you to communicate meaning to your audience and to interact with other performers on stage.
- **Physical skills for dance**
  You will work on a range of physical skills (e.g. balance, posture, coordination and alignment) to help develop your physical skills as a dancer and will be given the opportunity to improve these skills in workshops and rehearsals.
- **Movement reproduction and memory**
  The ability to reproduce movements accurately and remember them in phrases and longer routines is an important skill for any dancer. Your BTEC will allow you to improve these skills in a range of different dance contexts.

- **Interpretive skills for dance**
  Like actors, dancers need to interpret the story, mood and/or style of the piece they are to perform. In developing interpretive skills you will learn about focus, phrasing, projection, musicality, and facial and bodily expression.
- **Musical theatre skills**
  Musicals present particular challenges to performers, who are expected to combine acting, singing and dancing skills in their work. Your BTEC programme provides an opportunity to develop and improve these three skill areas in rehearsal and performance.
- **Singing skills**
  The BTEC National in Performing Arts will provide you with opportunity to develop skills in solo and ensemble singing through an understanding of vocal technique.

Personal, learning and thinking skills

Regardless of the pathway you are studying there are some essential personal, learning and thinking skills (PLTS) that you will develop while you are completing your BTEC programme. PLTS will be covered in more depth later on in this Study Skills Guide (see page 75).

Your own skills

Consider the performance-related skills described and carry out a quick skills audit using the grid below.

Which performance-related skills do you already have experience of?	
Which performance-related skills do you most want to develop and improve on your BTEC programme?	
Which personal, learning and thinking skills do you already possess?	
Which personal, learning and thinking skills do you most need to develop and improve?	

Step One: Understand your course and how it works

Case study: Where could the BTEC National in Performing Arts take you?

Andy is 16 and is about to begin a BTEC National in Performing Arts (Acting).

'I've been into performing since I was about 10, so I was really excited when I found out my local sixth form centre was offering a BTEC in Performing Arts. In some ways choosing to do the course was an easy decision, because I love everything to do with the theatre and my ambition is to work in the performing arts industry in some capacity in the future. I did, however, consider my options very carefully before I applied.

I had the opportunity to choose one of two pathways being taught – Musical Theatre and Acting. Having looked at the units I would study on each course I decided to apply to do the Acting pathway. This will give me the opportunity to develop my acting skills in a range of different projects including theatre in education, classical plays and devising. I did some devising work in GCSE Drama and really enjoyed it, so I am keen to do more.

Once I had made my decision I had to do an audition and take part in a group workshop. The audition was a bit scary but the workshop was great as it involved lots of different activities and drama games. I was really pleased when I was offered a place.

I know from what I have been told by the tutors that the next two years will be hard work. A few of my friends, who have opted for subjects such as science and humanities, have been joking and saying my course will just involve messing around but they couldn't be more wrong. The assignment programme looks quite daunting and I am concerned about how hard I will have to work to keep on top of all the deadlines. I know, however, that I have made a good decision and I can't wait to begin my course.'

Reflection points

- What were your reasons for joining your BTEC in Performing Arts programme?
- What are you most looking forward to on the programme?
- Is there anything you are concerned about?

Andy has selected the Acting pathway. Which pathway have you chosen? What affected your decision?

All BTEC Level 3 National qualifications are **vocational** or **work-related**. This means that you gain specific knowledge and understanding relevant to your chosen area. It gives you several advantages when you start work.

For example, you will already know quite a lot about your chosen area, which will help you settle down more quickly. If you are already employed, you become more valuable to your employer.

Your BTEC course will prepare you for the work you want to do.

There are four types of BTEC Level 3 National qualification: Certificates, Subsidiary Diplomas, Diplomas and Extended Diplomas

	Certificate	Subsidiary Diploma	Diploma	Extended Diploma
Credit	30	60	120	180
Equivalence	1 AS-level	1 A-level	2 A-levels	3 A-levels

These qualifications are often described as **nested**. This means that they fit inside each other (rather like Russian dolls) because the same units are common to each qualification – so you can progress from one to another easily by completing more units.

TOP TIP

The structure of BTEC Level 3 National qualifications means it's easy to progress from one type to another and gain more credits, as well as specialise in particular areas that interest you.

- Every BTEC Level 3 National qualification has a set number of **mandatory units** that all learners must complete.
- All BTEC Level 3 National qualifications include **optional units** that enable you to study particular areas in more depth.
- Some BTEC Level 3 National qualifications have **specialist pathways**, which may have additional mandatory units. These specialist pathways allow you to follow your career aims more precisely. For example, if you are studying to become an IT practitioner, you can choose pathways in Software Development, Networking, Systems Support or IT and Business.
- On all BTEC courses you are expected to be responsible for your own learning. Obviously your tutor will give you help and guidance when necessary but you also need to be 'self-starting' and able to use your own initiative. Ideally, you can also assess how well you are doing and make improvements when necessary.
- BTEC Level 3 National grades convert to UCAS points, just like A-levels, but the way you are assessed and graded on a BTEC course is different, as you will see in the next section.

Key points

- You can study part-time or full-time for your BTEC Level 3 National.
- You can do a Certificate, Subsidiary Diploma, Diploma, or Extended Diploma, and progress easily from one to the other.
- You will study both mandatory units and optional units on your course.
- When you have completed your BTEC course you can get a job (or **apprenticeship**), use your qualification to develop your career and/or continue studying to degree level.
- On all BTEC Level 3 National courses, the majority of your learning is practical and vocationally focused to develop the skills you need for your chosen career.

Using the Edexcel website to find out about your course

- You can check all the details about your BTEC Level 3 National course on the Edexcel website – go to www.edexcel.com.
- Enter the title of your BTEC Level 3 National qualification in the qualifications finder.
- Now find the specification in the list of documents. This is a long document so don't try to print it. Instead, look at the information on the units you will be studying to see the main topics you will cover.
- Then save the document or bookmark the page so that you can easily refer to it again if you need to.

Action points

1 By discussing with your tutor and by exploring the Edexcel website, find out the key information about your course and use it to complete the 'Important Information' form on the next page. You can refer to this form at any time to refresh your memory about any part of your studies.

a) Check whether you are studying for a BTEC Level 3 Certificate, Subsidiary Diploma, Diploma, or Extended Diploma and the number of units you will be studying.

b) Find out the titles of the mandatory units you will be studying.

c) Find out the titles of the optional units and identify the ones offered at your centre.

d) Check the length of your course, and when you will be studying each unit.

e) Identify the optional units you will be taking. On some National courses you will do this at the start, while on others you may make your final decision later.

f) Find out other relevant information about your BTEC Level 3 National qualification. Your centre may have already given you details about the structure.

g) Ask your tutor to help you to complete point 10 on the form. Depending on your course, you may be developing specific additional or personal skills – such as personal, learning and thinking skills (PLTS) and functional skills – or spending time on work experience, going on visits or doing other activities linked to your subject area.

h) Talk to your tutor about point 12 on the form as your sources of information will depend on the careers guidance and information at your centre. You may find it useful to exchange ideas with other members of your class.

IMPORTANT INFORMATION ON MY BTEC LEVEL 3 NATIONAL COURSE	
1	The title of the BTEC Level 3 National qualification I am studying is:
2	The length of my course is:
3	The total number of units I will study is:
4	The number of mandatory units I have to study is:
5	The titles of these mandatory units and the dates (or terms) when I will study them are:
6	The main topics I will learn in each mandatory unit include:

	IMPORTANT INFORMATION ON MY BTEC LEVEL 3 NATIONAL COURSE
7	The number of optional units I have to study is:
8	The titles of the optional units I will study are:
9	The main topics I will learn in each optional unit include:
10	Other important aspects of my course are:
11	After I have achieved my BTEC Level 3 National my options include:
12	Useful sources of information I can use to find out more about these options include:

2 Many learners already have information, contacts or direct experiences that relate to their course. For example, you may have a specific interest or hobby that links to a unit, such as being a St John Ambulance cadet if you are studying Public Services. Think about the relevant sources of information you already have access to and complete the table below.

MY INFORMATION SOURCES	
Experts I know	(Who they are, what they know)
My hobbies and interests	(What they are, what they involve)
My job(s)	(Past and present work and work experience, and what I did)
Programmes I like to watch	(What these are, how they relate to my course)
Magazines and/or books I read	(What these are, examples of relevant articles)
ICT sources	(My centre's intranet as well as useful websites)
Other	(Other sources relevant for my particular course and the topics I will be studying)

Activity: Your future options

At the beginning of a new course it is helpful to think about what options may be available to you for your career pathway in performing arts. All assignments and work experience on the programme contribute to your final grade and knowing what you are aiming for will help keep you motivated.

Using a mind map to explore different ideas is a way for you to start to consider the range of options available to you and what you will need to follow each career pathway.

For example, if you wish to work in the theatre, you could explore the different routes to joining a theatre company.

You will find the Internet a useful source of information. A good starting point is the website of your local amateur dramatics society.

Create a mind map on the next page to record your ideas.

TOP TIP

People usually perform better if they understand why they have chosen, or been asked, to do something.

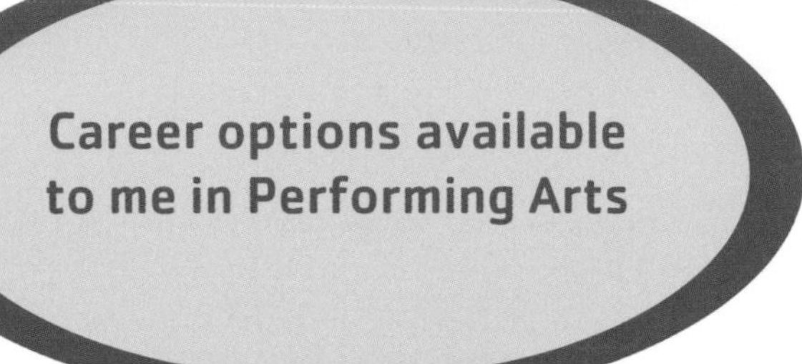
Career options available
to me in Performing Arts

Step Two: Understand how you are assessed and graded

Case study: BTEC assignments

Kev looks back at the assessed work he completed in his first term on the BTEC National.

'During the first term of the course we completed two assignments. One was for Unit 3: Performing Arts Business. I had to research employment opportunities in the performing arts industry to find out about their functions and responsibilities. The research took quite a while. I spent some time in the college library and also searched for relevant articles on the Internet. I managed to interview Dane, who teaches part-time at the college and also works as an actor for a local theatre company. I gathered some really useful information from him so I have decided to try to include some first-hand or primary research when I am completing similar research-based assignments in the future.

As everybody in the class had researched different roles we presented the results of our investigations to each other using PowerPoint. It was a bit stressful, but it meant we were able to share all the information we had gathered.

The other assignment was much bigger and covered parts of the Theatre for Children and Principles of Acting units. The tutor explained that this is known as an integrated assignment as it integrates learning outcomes from more than one unit. We had to work as a theatre company to produce a children's show to be toured into primary schools. We were given 8 weeks to complete the assignment but it was still hard work to get everything done in time.

This assignment was different from the other one because I had to work as part of a team, rather than individually. I felt a real responsibility to do well, not just for myself but also for the sake of the others in my class. Our tutor videoed some of the rehearsal sessions, as well as the performance, and we were asked to keep an actor's log to record the work that was done and the decisions made. The final performances were great fun and it made all the hard work worthwhile.'

Reflection points

- Which of the two assignments do you think is the most challenging?
- What kinds of skills and knowledge are being assessed by each? Are any skills common to both assignments?
- In one of Kev's assignments he worked individually, in the other he worked as a member of a team. Do you think you work better on your own or as part of a group? How could you improve your skills in the weaker area?

Your assessment

This section looks at the importance of your assignments, how they are graded and how this converts into unit points and UCAS points. Unlike A-levels, there are no externally-set final exams on a BTEC course. Even if you know this because you already have a BTEC First qualification, you should still read this section as now you will be working at a different level.

Your learning is assessed by **assignments**, set by your tutors. You will complete these throughout your course, using many different **assessment methods**, such as real-life case studies, **projects** and presentations. Some assignments may be work-based or **time-constrained** – it depends very much on the vocational area you are studying.

Your assignments are based on **learning outcomes** set by Edexcel. These are listed for each unit in your course specification. You must achieve **all** the learning outcomes to pass each unit.

TOP TIP

Check the learning outcomes for each unit by referring to the course specification – go to www.edexcel.com.

Important skills to help you achieve your grades include:

- researching and analysing information (see page 53)
- using your time effectively (see page 25)
- working co-operatively as a member of a team (see page 47.)

Your grades, unit points and UCAS points

On a BTEC Level 3 National course, assessments that meet the learning outcomes are graded as pass, merit or distinction. The different grades within each unit are set out by Edexcel as **grading criteria** in a **grading grid**. These criteria identify the **higher-level skills** you must demonstrate to achieve a higher grade (see also Step Six – Understand your assessment, on page 35).

All your assessment grades earn **unit points**. The total points you get for all your units determines your final qualification grade(s) – pass, merit or distinction. You get:

- one final grade if you are taking a Certificate or Subsidiary Diploma
- two final grades if you are taking a Diploma
- three final grades if you are taking an Extended Diploma.

Your points and overall grade(s) convert to **UCAS points**, which you need to be accepted onto a degree course. For example, if you achieve three final pass grades for your BTEC Level 3 Extended Diploma, you get 120 UCAS Tariff points. If you achieve three final distinction grades, this increases to 360 – equivalent to three GCE A-levels.

Please note that all UCAS information was correct at the time of going to print, but we would advise that you check their website for the most up to date information. See page 94 for how to access their website.

Case study: Securing a university place

Chris and Shaheeda both want a university place and have worked hard on their BTEC Level 3 Extended Diploma course.

Chris's final score is 226 unit points, which converts to 280 UCAS Tariff points. Shaheeda has a total score of 228 unit points – just two points more – which converts to 320 UCAS points! This is because a score of between 204 and 227 unit points gives 280 UCAS points, whereas a score of 228 to 251 points gives 320 UCAS points.

Shaheeda is delighted because this increases her chances of getting a place on the degree course she wants. Chris is annoyed. He says if he had realised he would have worked harder on his last assignment to get two points more.

You start to earn points from your first assessment, so you get many benefits from settling in quickly and doing good work from the start. Understanding how **grade boundaries** work also helps you to focus your efforts to get the best possible final grade.

You will be able to discuss your learning experiences, your personal progress and the achievement of your learning objectives in **individual tutorials** with your tutor. These enable you to monitor your progress and overcome temporary difficulties. You can also talk about any worries you have. Your tutor is one of your most important resources and a tutorial gives you their undivided attention.

You can talk through any questions or problems in your tutorials.

Key points

- Your learning is assessed in a variety of ways, such as by assignments, projects and real-life case studies.
- You need to demonstrate specific knowledge and skills to achieve the learning outcomes set by Edexcel. You must achieve all the grading criteria to pass a unit.
- The grading criteria for pass, merit and distinction are shown in a grading grid for the unit. Higher-level skills are needed for higher grades.
- The assessment grades of pass, merit and distinction convert to unit points. The total unit points you receive for the course determines your final overall grade(s) and UCAS points.

TOP TIP

It's always tempting to spend longer on work you like doing and are good at, but focusing on improving your weak areas will do more to boost your overall grade(s).

Action points

1 Find out more about your own course by carrying out this activity.

a) Find the learning outcomes for the units you are currently studying. Your tutor may have given you these, or you can find them in your course specification – go to www.edexcel.com and search for your qualification.

b) Look at the grading grid for the units and identify the way the requirements change for the higher grades. If there are some unfamiliar words, check these in Step Six of this guide (see page 35 onwards).

c) If the unit points system still seems complicated, ask your tutor to explain it.

d) Check the UCAS points you would need for the course or university which interests you.

e) Design a form you can use to record the unit points you earn throughout your course. Keep this up-to-date. Regularly check how your points relate to your overall grade(s), based on the grade boundaries for your qualification. Your tutor can give you this information or you can check it yourself in the course specification.

Activity: Keeping track of your assessments

It is very important that you keep track of the assessment requirements of your programme so you can plan your time to meet deadlines and keep track of what has been completed in terms of the units and their learning outcomes.

Find out about the assignments that will be set during the first term of your course and enter the details on the table below.

Use the final column to tick off assignments when they have been completed.

Title of assignment	Unit(s) and learning outcomes covered	Assessment methods	Hand in/ completion date	Completed?
e.g. Job Opportunities in the Performing Arts	Unit 3: Performing Arts Business LO 1	Oral presentation to class	25 November 2010	✓

Step Three: Understand yourself

Case study: Being self-aware

Many people have the impression that anyone who is involved in the performing arts will have a loud and outgoing personality and enjoy being the centre of attention. While some of these personality traits might be useful to someone wanting work in the industry they are not the only qualities needed to succeed on a Performing Arts course.

Take Kym and Huw. Both are studying on a BTEC National in Performing Arts course, but they have very different personalities.

Kym loves to be in the spotlight and enjoys the many practical workshops and performances her programme has to offer. She is a talented dancer and singer and is keen to pursue a career in musical theatre. She excels in performance activities, but has to work harder when completing written work. Kym can also be rather overbearing when completing group tasks and tends to go with her gut instinct when coming up with ideas rather than trying several out. She also gets easily frustrated in dance classes with those who are less experienced than she is.

Huw, on the other hand, is a more quiet and thoughtful person. He is well organised and very supportive of others in the group. These are also vital skills for someone working in the performing arts industry. Huw is creative and likes research activities, which means he does particularly well in assignments that involve devising new performance material or analysing characters in a scripted piece. However, Huw is not as assertive as he could be, particularly when working as part of a team. He sometimes takes too much of a back seat when decisions are made and is not forceful enough when it comes to getting the group to consider his ideas.

Reflection points

- How aware do you think you are of your own personality traits?
- Do you recognise any of your own personality traits in Kym and/or Huw?
- What personality traits do you have that will be useful to you on your course?
- Do you have any that might cause problems?

Self-awareness means understanding how you 'tick'. For example, do you prefer practical activities rather than theory? Do you prefer to draw or sketch an idea, rather than write about it?

Self-awareness is important as it makes you less reliant on other people's opinions and gives you confidence in your own judgement. You can also reflect on your actions to learn from your experiences.

Self-awareness also means knowing your own strengths and weaknesses. Knowing your strengths enables you to feel positive and confident about yourself and your abilities. Knowing your weaknesses means you know the areas you need to develop.

You can analyse yourself by looking at...

... your personality and preferences

You may have taken a personality test at your centre. If not, your tutor may recommend one to use, or there are many available online.

Many employers ask job candidates to complete a personality test so that they can match the type of work they are offering to the most suitable candidates. Although these tests can only give a broad indication of someone's personality they may help to avoid mismatches, such as hiring someone who is introverted to work in sales.

... your skills and abilities

To succeed in your assignments, and to progress in a career, requires a number of skills. Some may be vocationally specific, or professional, skills that you can improve during your course – such as sporting performance on a Sports course. Others are broader skills that are invaluable no matter what you are studying – such as communicating clearly and co-operating with others.

You will work faster and more accurately, and have greater confidence, if you are skilled and proficient. A quick skills check will identify any problem areas.

TOP TIP

Use the Skills Building section on page 75 to identify the skills you need for your course. You'll also find hints and tips for improving any weak areas.

Key points

- You need certain skills and abilities to get the most out of your BTEC Level 3 National course and to develop your career potential.
- Knowing your strengths and weaknesses is a sign of maturity. It gives you greater confidence in your abilities and enables you to focus on areas for improvement.

TOP TIP

You will find more help on developing your skills and abilities in the sections on: Working as a member of a group; Using time wisely; Researching and analysing information; and Making effective presentations.

Action points

1 Gain insight into your own personality by answering each of the following statements *True* or *False* with a tick. Be honest!

		True	False
a)	If someone annoys me, I can tell them about it without causing offence.		
b)	If someone is talking, I often interrupt them to give them my opinion.		
c)	I get really stressed if I'm under pressure.		
d)	I can sometimes become very emotional and upset on other people's behalf.		
e)	I sometimes worry that I can't cope and may make a mess of something.		
f)	I am usually keen, enthusiastic and motivated to do well.		
g)	I enjoy planning and organising my work.		
h)	I find it easy to work and co-operate with other people and take account of their opinions.		
i)	I am easily influenced by other people.		
j)	I often jump to conclusions and judge people and situations on first impressions.		
k)	I prefer to rely on facts and experience rather than following my instincts.		

Now identify which of the skills and qualities in the box below will be really important in your chosen career.

tact truthfulness listening skills
staying calm under pressure
empathy with others self-confidence
initiative planning and organising
working with others self-assurance
objective judgements

Use your answers to identify areas you should work on to be successful in the future.

2 As part of the UCAS process, all **higher education** applicants have to write a personal statement. This is different from a CV, which is a summary of achievements that all job applicants prepare. You may have already prepared a CV but not thought about a personal statement. Now is your chance to!

Read the information about personal statement in the box. Then answer these questions:

a) Explain why personal statements are so important for higher education applicants.

b) Why do you think it is important for your personal statement to read well and be error-free?

c) Suggest three reasons why you shouldn't copy a pre-written statement you have found online.

d) Check the websites you can access from the hotlink given in the box to see what to include in the statement and how to set it out.

e) Prepare a bullet point list of ten personal facts. Focus on your strengths and good reasons why you should be given a place on the higher education course of your choice. If possible, discuss your list with your tutor. Then keep it safely, as it will be useful if you need to write a personal statement later.

Personal statements

This is the information that all higher education applicants have to put in the blank space on their UCAS form. The aim is to sell yourself to admissions tutors. It can be pretty scary, especially if you haven't written anything like it before.

So, where do you start?

First, *never* copy pre-written statements you find online. These are just for guidance. Even worse are websites that offer to write your statement for a fee, and send you a few general, pre-written paragraphs. Forget them all: you can do better!

Imagine you are an admissions tutor with 60 places to offer to 200 applicants. What will you need to read in a personal statement to persuade you to offer the applicant a place?

Most likely, clear explanations about:

- what the applicant can contribute to the course
- why the applicant really wants a place on your course
- what the applicant has done to further his/her own interests in this area, eg voluntary work
- attributes that show this applicant would be a definite bonus – such as innovative ideas, with evidence eg 'I organised a newsletter which we published every three months ...'

A personal statement should be well written, with no grammatical or spelling errors and organised into clear paragraphs.

There are a number of helpful websites. To find out how to access them, go to page 86.

Activity: Keeping a record of your work

If you are applying for a place on a higher education course in performing or production arts, admissions tutors will be interested in the experience you have gained while working on productions, whether as part of your BTEC programme or during extra-curricular activities and work with amateur theatre or dance groups.

While it is not necessary to list all of these in a personal statement you should describe and discuss some typical examples of the experience you have gained.

During your time on your BTEC programme you should keep a record of the productions, shows, concerts, etc. you have contributed to and taken part in.

You should

- note the title of the production (and the playwright/composer if applicable)
- note the performance date(s)
- provide a brief description of the production and the company
- describe your role and responsibilities.

For example:

Production	Date	Company	Role/responsibilities
'The Visit' by Friedrich Dürrenmatt	12–14 Nov 2010	Southmoor Community College Youth Theatre	Assistant Stage Manager Prop Maker
'Cinderella' Devised by company	17–19 Dec 2010	Devonshire Amateur Dramatic Group	Buttons

Use or adapt the grid below to keep a record of your own work.

Production	Date	Company	Role/responsibilities

TOP TIPS

A very important aspect of being a performer is having a positive 'can do' attitude to life.

Step Four: Use your time wisely

Case study: Getting the balance right

Becky reflects on her organisational skills

'I've never been very well organised. If something can be put off until later I'm always very tempted to do so, but when I started my BTEC National I had really good intentions when it came to keeping up with the work. When we started work on our first performance project we were told that we should complete our actor's log as soon as possible after every session while the work completed was still fresh in our minds.

For the first few weeks I was really well organised and filled in my log as soon as I got in from college each day. But then I started to leave it until later so I could watch the TV or just hang around with my mates. I would promise myself that I'd catch up with it later in the evening or tomorrow or the next day. Before long my log was several weeks behind and, with a milestone assessment approaching, I had to go over my rough notes and try to think back to what we had done in each session. I ended up in a big panic and it me took ages to get everything up to date, much longer than it would have done if I'd just got on with it after each session as my tutor had suggested.

I didn't want to go through all that again so for my second project my goal was to complete my log as soon as I got home, no matter what. I got into the routine of grabbing a drink from the fridge, sitting down and getting on with it. When it was done I still had most of the evening to myself and I enjoyed my free time more knowing I was up to date with my work. When it came to handing my log in all I had to do was check it though and the bonus was that I ended up getting better grades for the project.'

Reflection points

- Do you ever put things off until another day and end up rushing at the last minute?
- How do you think you could incorporate homework, assignment and general organisational tasks into your daily/weekly routine? Make a plan and try to stick to it.
- What commitments do you have outside you course? How will you balance them with the requirements of your BTEC programme?

Most learners have to combine course commitments with other responsibilities such as a job (either full- or part-time) and family responsibilities. You will also want to see your friends and keep up your hobbies and interests. Juggling these successfully means you need to be able to use your time wisely.

This involves planning what to do and when to do it to prevent panics about unexpected deadlines. As your course progresses, this becomes even more important as your workload may increase towards the end of a term. In some cases there could be two or more assignments to complete simultaneously. Although tutors try to avoid clashes of this sort, it is sometimes inevitable.

To cope successfully, you need time-management skills, in particular:

- how to organise your time to be more productive
- how to prioritise tasks
- how to overcome time-wasters.

Organising your time

- **Use a diary or wall chart.**
  Using a different colour pen for each, enter:
  - your course commitments, eg assignment dates, tutorials, visits
  - important personal commitments, eg sports matches, family birthdays
  - your work commitments.

TOP TIP

A diary is useful because you can update it as you go, but a wall chart gives you a better overview of your commitments over several weeks. Keep your diary or chart up-to-date and check ahead regularly so that you have prior warning of important dates.

- **Identify how you currently use your time.**
  - Work out how much time you spend at your centre, at work, at home and on social activities.
  - Identify which commitments are vital and which are optional so you can find extra time if necessary.
- **Plan and schedule future commitments.**
  - Write down any appointments and tasks you must do.
  - Enter assignment review dates and final deadline dates in different colours.
  - This should stop you from arranging a dental appointment on the same morning that you are due to give an important presentation – or planning a hectic social life when you have lots of course work to do.
- **Decide your best times for doing course work.**
  - Expect to do most of your course work in your own time.
  - Work at the time of day when you feel at your best.
  - Work regularly, and in relatively short bursts, rather than once or twice a week for very long stretches.
  - If you're a night owl, allow an hour to 'switch off' before you go to bed.
- **Decide where to work.**
  - Choose somewhere you can concentrate without interruption.
  - Make sure there is space for resources you use, such as books or specialist equipment.
  - You also need good lighting and a good – but not too comfortable – chair.
  - If you can't find suitable space at home, check out your local or college library.
- **Assemble the items you need.**
  - Book ahead to get specific books, journals or DVDs from the library.
  - Ensure you have your notes, handouts and assignment brief with you.
  - Use sticky notes to mark important pages in textbooks or folders.

TOP TIP

Set yourself a target when you start work, so that you feel positive and productive at the end. Always try to end a session when a task is going well, rather than when you are stuck. Then you will be keener to go back to it the next day. Note down outstanding tasks you need to continue with next time.

- **Plan ahead**
  - If anything is unclear about an assignment, ask your tutor for an explanation as soon as you can.
  - Break down long tasks or assignments into manageable chunks, eg find information, decide what to use, create a plan for finished work, write rough draft of first section, etc.
  - Work back from deadline dates so that you allow plenty of time to do the work.
  - Always allow more time than you need. It is better to finish early than to run out of time.

TOP TIP

If you are working on a task as a group, organise and agree times to work together. Make sure you have somewhere to meet where you can work without disturbing other courses or groups.

- **Be self-disciplined.**
  - Don't put things off because you're not in the mood. Make it easier by doing simple tasks first to get a sense of achievement. Then move on to something harder.
  - Plan regular breaks. If you're working hard you need a change of activity to recharge your batteries.
  - If you have a serious problem or personal crisis, talk to your personal tutor promptly.

TOP TIP

Make sure you know the consequences of missing an assignment deadline, as well as the dispensations and exemptions that can be given if you have an unavoidable and serious problem, such as illness (see also page 73).

How to prioritise tasks

Prioritising means doing the most important and urgent task first. Normally this will be the task or assignment with the closest deadline or the one that will most affect your overall course grades.

One way of prioritising is to group tasks into ABC categories.

Category A tasks	These must be done now as they are very important and cannot be delayed, eg completing an assignment to be handed in tomorrow.
Category B tasks	These are jobs you should do if you have time, because otherwise they will rapidly become Category A, eg getting a book that you need for your next assignment.
Category C tasks	These are tasks you should do if you have the time, eg rewriting notes jotted down quickly in a lesson.

Expect to be flexible. For example, if you need to allow time for information to arrive, then send for this first. If you are working in a team, take into account other people's schedules when you are making arrangements.

Overcoming time-wasters

Everyone has days when they don't know where the time has gone. It may be because they were constantly interrupted or because things just kept going wrong. Whatever the reason, the end result is that some jobs don't get done.

If this happens to you regularly, you need to take steps to keep on track.

Some useful tips are:

- **Warn people in advance when you will be working.**
  - Ask them to not interrupt you.
  - If you are in a separate room, shut the door. If someone comes in, make it clear you don't want to talk.
  - If that doesn't work, find somewhere else (or some other time) to work.
- **Switch off your mobile, TV, radio and iPod/ MP3 player.**
  - Don't respond to, or make, calls or texts.
  - If someone rings your home phone, let voicemail answer or ask them to call back later.
- **Be strict with yourself when you are working online.**
  - Don't check your email until you've finished work.
  - Don't get distracted when searching for information.
  - Keep away from social networking sites.
- **Avoid displacement activities.**
  - These are the normally tedious jobs, such as cleaning your computer screen, that suddenly seem far more attractive than working!

TOP TIP

Benefits to managing your own time include being less stressed (because you are not reacting to problems or crises), producing better work and having time for a social life.

Talking to friends can occupy a lot of time.

TOP TIP

The first step in managing your own time is learning to say 'no' (nicely!) if someone asks you to do something tempting when you should be working.

Key points

- Being in control of your time allows you to balance your commitments according to their importance and means you won't let anyone down.
- Organising yourself and your time involves knowing how you spend your time now, planning when and where it is best to work, scheduling commitments and setting sensible timescales to complete your work.
- Knowing how to prioritise means you will schedule work effectively according to its urgency and importance. You will need self-discipline to follow the schedule you have set for yourself.
- Identifying ways in which you may waste time means you can guard against these to achieve your goals more easily.

Action points

1 Start planning your time properly.

a) Find out how many assignments you will have this term, and when you will get them. Put this information into your diary or planner.

b) Update this with your other commitments for the term – both work/course-related and social. Identify possible clashes and decide how to resolve the problem.

c) Identify one major task or assignment you will do soon. Divide it into manageable chunks and decide how long to allow for each chunk, plus some spare time for any problems. If possible, check your ideas with your tutor before you put them into your planner.

2 How good are you at being responsible for your own learning?

a) Fill in the following table. Score yourself out of 5 for each area: where 0 is awful and 5 is excellent. Ask a friend or relative to score you as well. See if you can explain any differences.

	Scoring yourself	Other person's score for you
Being punctual		
Organisational ability		
Tidiness		
Working accurately		
Finding and correcting own mistakes		
Solving problems		
Accepting responsibility		
Working with details		
Planning how to do a job		
Using own initiative		
Thinking up new ideas		
Meeting deadlines		

b) Draw up your own action plan for areas where you need to improve. If possible, talk this through at your next **tutorial** (see page 90).

TOP TIPS

Don't waste time doing things that distract you when studying for this course. In a performing arts company, time costs money.

Activity: Performing Arts Productions – Keeping track of rehearsals and performances

On a performing arts programme there will be times when the amount of commitment in terms of hours will increase. This is likely to be the case when you are preparing for and taking part in the public performances that are an integral part of this vocational course.

When you are working on a production you may be required to attend your centre in the evening and/or at weekends to take part in rehearsals, production week activities and performances. This is an important part of your course and reflects the way in which professionals in the industry work.

It is important that you find out the dates of any rehearsals and performances so you can plan ahead, for instance getting time off from evening or weekend jobs and making arrangements for travel.

Use the grid below to record details of productions you will be taking part in. Include the dates of the performances and details of final rehearsals, as well as when production week activities will be taking place (usually the week before the performance).

Title of or description of production	Dates of final rehearsals/ production week activities	Dates of performances

Step Five: Utilise all your resources

Case study: Using your resources

Learners on a BTEC National in Performing Arts are often described as being their own resource and you will certainly depend on your fellow learners when completing the group projects and assignments you will be set.

Depending on the pathway you are studying on your BTEC National in Performing Arts, you will also need to use a range of physical resources and equipment to complete your course.

- Jenni is a learner on the dance pathway. She has a dance kit consisting of leggings and a t-shirt with her college's logo on it. It is important that she has her kit for every practical session she takes part in. Shoes are also important for a dancer. Jenni wears jazz shoes for some classes and has recently invested in a pair of tap shoes as she has opted for a tap dance unit in her second term.
- Mark is a musical theatre student at the same college. He also needs a dance kit although for the boys the leggings are replaced by sweatpants. He gets guitar lessons as an extra part of his course and needs to make sure his instrument is always in good working order and that he carries spare strings.
- Rianna is an acting student. She has a 'uniform' consisting of black sweatpants and a t-shirt. This is because neutral dress helps actors to become like a blank canvas onto which characters can be drawn.
- Joseph is a production student and much of the resources and equipment he uses is supplied by the college in the workshops and back stage areas in which he works. During theatre productions there is, however, a dress code for those working back stage, who must wear black or dark clothing.

Reflection points

- Why do you think it is important for learners taking part in practical sessions to wear specific clothing and/or footwear?
- Do you think neutral dress helps when approaching acting projects?
- Why do you think those working backstage need to wear dark-coloured clothes?

Your resources are all the things that can help you to be successful in your BTEC Level 3 National qualification, from your favourite website to your study buddy (see page 32) who collects handouts for you if you miss a class.

Your centre will provide essential resources, such as a library with appropriate books and electronic reference sources, the computer network and internet access. You will have to provide basic resources such as pens, pencils and file folders yourself. If you have to buy your own textbooks, look after them carefully so you can sell them on at the end of your course.

Here is a list of resources, with tips for getting the best out of them.

- **Course information**. This includes your course specification, this Study Skills Guide and all information on the Edexcel website relating to your BTEC Level 3 National course. Course information from your centre will include term dates, assignment dates and your timetable. Keep everything safely so you can refer to it whenever you need to clarify something.
- **Course materials**. These include course handouts, printouts, your own notes and textbooks. Put handouts into an A4 folder as soon as you get them. Use a separate folder for each unit you study.

TOP TIP

Filing notes and handouts promptly means they don't get lost, will stay clean and uncrumpled and you won't waste time looking for them.

- **Stationery**. You need pens and pencils, a notepad, a hole puncher, a stapler and sets of dividers. Dividers should be clearly labelled to help you store and quickly find notes, printouts and handouts. Your notes should be headed and dated, and those from your own research must also include your source (see Step Eight – page 53 onwards.)
- **People**. Your tutors, specialist staff at college, classmates, your employer and work colleagues, your relatives and friends are all valuable resources. Many will have particular skills or work in the vocational area that you are studying. Talking to other learners can help to clarify issues that there may not have been time to discuss fully in class.

  A **study buddy** is another useful resource as they can make notes and collect handouts if you miss a session. (Remember to return the favour when they are away.)

Always be polite when you are asking people for information. Prepare the questions first and remember that you are asking for help, not trying to get them to do the work for you! If you are interviewing someone for an assignment or project, good preparations are vital. (See Step Eight – page 53 onwards.)

If someone who did the course before you offers help, be careful. It is likely the course requirements will have changed. Never be tempted to copy their assignments (or someone else's). This is **plagiarism** – a deadly sin in the educational world (see also Step Six – page 36.)

TOP TIP

A positive attitude, an enquiring mind and the ability to focus on what is important will have a major impact on your final result.

Key points

- Resources help you to achieve your qualification. Find out what resources you have available to you and use them wisely.
- Have your own stationery items.
- Know how to use central facilities and resources such as the library, learning resource centres and your computer network. Always keep to the policy on IT use in your centre.
- People are a key resource – school or college staff, work colleagues, members of your class, friends, family and people who are experts in their field.

Action points

1 a) List the resources you will need to complete your course successfully. Identify which ones will be provided by your school or college, and which you need to supply yourself.

b) Go through your list again and identify the resources you already have (or know how to access) and those you don't.

c) Compare your list with a friend's and decide how to obtain and access the resources you need. Add any items to your list that you forgot.

d) List the items you still need to get and set a target date for doing this.

2 'Study buddy' schemes operate in many centres. Find out if this applies to your own centre and how you can make the best use of it.

In some you can choose your study buddy, in others people are paired up by their tutor.

- Being a study buddy might mean just collecting handouts when the other person is absent, and giving them important news.
- It may also mean studying together and meeting (or keeping contact by phone or email) to exchange ideas and share resources.

With a study buddy you can share resources and stay on top of the course if you're ever away.

Activity: Dressing appropriately

Find out from your tutor about any rules regarding how you should dress and present yourselves for particular sessions. Many of these rules will be in place for health and safety reasons, for instance wearing a particular kind of footwear when undertaking physical activities such as dance sessions or wearing a hard hat when lights are being rigged. Some rules, however, may be for professional reasons, for example to ensure all members of an acting or dance company adopt the company identity when working together. There may be rules regarding the wearing of jewellery and having hair tied back for certain sessions.

It is important you know and understand all these rules before you begin working. Make a list of any regulations in terms of dress, footwear and physical appearance for the types of sessions you will be involved in using the table below.

Type of session	Rules
e.g. Contemporary dance classes	e.g. dress – black leggings and t-shirt for girls; sweat pants and t-shirt for boys. Hair must be tied back if longer than shoulder length. Small earrings allowed (e.g. studs or small sleepers) otherwise no jewellery. No shoes allowed in the dance studio.

Step Six: Understand your assessment

Case study: Gaining the marks you need

Aleesha reflects on the time she was given her first assignment.

'When I was given my first assignment brief I was really nervous. It was quite an official looking document and I thought, "This is it. The fun is over!"

It was actually really easy to understand what the assignment brief was asking me to do once our tutor had gone over it. It was really helpful to have all the information I needed about the project in one piece.

The brief told me

- what I was expected to do
- the type of evidence I needed to hand in
- when the various tasks had to be completed.

As the first assignment was mostly practical there wasn't much to hand in. We were assessed on our contribution to dance workshops over a period of time and we were observed by our tutor, who also took some video recordings of our work at various milestones in the project. It really made me work hard knowing I was being assessed on my work in every session. I also had to keep a log of the techniques we were learning and the progress I made each week. The log had to be handed in at the end of the project.

I am now used to getting and completing assignments. Because each brief is set out in the same way it is very easy now for me to understand what is required of me.'

Reflection points

- Ask your tutor to show you an example of an assignment from your BTEC programme. What are your first thoughts when looking at it?
- How easy do you think it is to find and understand the important information?

Being successful on any BTEC Level 3 National course means first understanding what you must do in your assignments – and then doing it.

Your assignments focus on topics you have already covered in class. If you've attended regularly, you should be able to complete them confidently.

However, there are some common pitfalls it's worth thinking about. Here are tips to avoid them:

- Read the instructions (the assignment brief) properly and several times before you start.
- Make sure you understand what you are supposed to do. Ask if anything is unclear.
- Complete every part of a task. If you ignore a question, you can't meet the grading criteria.
- Prepare properly. Do your research or reading before you start. Don't guess the answers.
- Communicate your ideas clearly. You can check this by asking someone who doesn't know the subject to look at your work.
- Only include relevant information. Padding out answers makes it look as if you don't know your subject.
- Do the work earlier rather than later to avoid any last-minute panics.
- Pay attention to advice and feedback that your tutor has given you.

TOP TIP

Most learners don't do their best in assessments because of silly mistakes, carelessness and rushed work, rather than through major problems of understanding. Make sure you take the time to plan and understand your assignments.

The assignment 'brief'

This may be longer than its name implies! The assignment brief includes all the instructions for an assignment and several other details, as you can see in the table below.

What will you find in a BTEC Level 3 National assignment brief?	
Content	**Details**
Title	This will link to the unit and learning outcomes
Format/style	Written assignment, presentation, demonstration, etc
Preparation	Read case study, do research, etc
Learning outcomes	These state the knowledge you must demonstrate to obtain a required grade
Grading criterion/ criteria covered	eg P1/M1/D1
Individual/group work	Remember to identify your own contribution in any group work
Feedback	Tutor, peer review
Interim review dates	Dates to see your tutor
Final deadline	Last submission date

TOP TIP

Reading and understanding each assignment brief is vital. Ask your tutor if there's anything you don't understand.

Your centre's rules and regulations

Your centre will have several policies and guidelines about assignments, which you need to check carefully. Many, such as those listed below, relate to Edexcel policies and guidelines.

- The procedure to follow if you have a serious problem and can't meet a deadline. An extension may be granted.
- The penalty for missing a deadline without good reason.
- The penalty for copying someone else's work. This is usually severe, so never share your work (or CDs or USB flash drive) with anyone else, and don't borrow theirs.
- **Plagiarism** is also serious misconduct. This means copying someone's work (see also page 32) or quoting from books and websites and pretending it is your own work.
- The procedure to follow if you disagree with the grade you are given.

Understanding the question or task

There are two aspects to a question or task. The first is the **command words**, which are described below. The second is the **presentation instructions**, which is what you are asked to do – don't write a report when you should be producing a chart!

Command words such as 'explain', 'describe', 'analyse', 'evaluate' state how a question must be answered. You may be asked to 'describe' something at pass level, but you will need to do more, perhaps 'analyse' or 'evaluate', to achieve merit or distinction.

Many learners fail to achieve higher grades because they don't realise the difference between these words. Instead of analysing or evaluating they give an explanation instead. Adding more details won't achieve a higher grade – you need to change your whole approach to the answer.

The **grading grid** for each unit of your course gives you the command words, so that you know what to do to achieve a pass, merit or distinction. The tables that follow show you what is usually required when you see a particular command word. These are just examples to guide you as the exact response will depend on the question. If you have any doubts, check with your tutor before you start work.

There are two important points to note:

- A command word, such as 'create' or 'explain', may be repeated in the grading criteria for different grades. In these cases the complexity or range of the task itself increases at the higher grades.
- Command words vary depending on your vocational area. So Art and Design grading grids may use different command words from Applied Science, for example.

TOP TIP

Look at this section again when you get your first assignment and check the command words against these explanations.

To obtain a pass grade

To achieve a pass you must usually demonstrate that you understand the important facts relating to a topic and can state these clearly and concisely.

Command words for a pass	Meaning
Create (or produce)	Make, invent or construct an item.
Describe	Give a clear, straightforward description that includes all the main points and links these together logically.
Define	Clearly explain what a particular term means and give an example, if appropriate, to show what you mean.
Explain … how/why	Set out in detail the meaning of something, with reasons. It is often helpful to give an example of what you mean. Start with the topic then give the 'how' or 'why'.
Identify	Distinguish and state the main features or basic facts relating to a topic.
Interpret	Define or explain the meaning of something.
Illustrate	Give examples to show what you mean.
List	Provide the information required in a list rather than in continuous writing.
Outline	Write a clear description that includes all the main points but avoid going into too much detail.
Plan (or devise)	Work out and explain how you would carry out a task or activity.
Select (and present) information	Identify relevant information to support the argument you are making and communicate this in an appropriate way.
State	Write a clear and full account.
Undertake	Carry out a specific activity.
Examples: Identify the main features on a digital camera. Outline the steps to take to carry out research for an assignment.	

To obtain a merit grade

To obtain a merit you must prove that you can apply your knowledge in a specific way.

Command words for a merit	Meaning
Analyse	Identify separate factors, say how they relate to each other and how each one relates to the topic.
Classify	Sort your information into appropriate categories before presenting or explaining it.
Compare and contrast	Identify the main factors that apply in two or more situations and explain the similarities and differences or advantages and disadvantages.
Demonstrate	Provide several relevant examples or appropriate evidence which support the arguments you are making. In some vocational areas this may also mean giving a practical performance.
Discuss	Provide a thoughtful and logical argument to support the case you are making.
Explain (in detail)	Provide details and give reasons and/or evidence to clearly support the argument you are making.
Implement	Put into practice or operation. You may also have to interpret or justify the effect or result.
Interpret	Understand and explain an effect or result.
Justify	Give appropriate reasons to support your opinion or views and show how you arrived at these conclusions.
Relate/report	Give a full account, with reasons.
Research	Carry out a full investigation.
Specify	Provide full details and descriptions of selected items or activities.
Examples: Compare and contrast the performance of two different digital cameras. Explain in detail the steps to take to research an assignment.	

To obtain a distinction grade

To obtain a distinction you must prove that you can make a reasoned judgement based on appropriate evidence.

Command words for a distinction	Meaning
Analyse	Identify the key factors, show how they are linked and explain the importance and relevance of each.
Assess	Give careful consideration to all the factors or events that apply and identify which are the most important and relevant, with reasons.
Comprehensively explain	Give a very detailed explanation that covers all the relevant points and give reasons for your views or actions.
Critically comment	Give your view after you have considered all the evidence, particularly the importance of both the relevant positive and negative aspects.
Evaluate	Review the information and then bring it together to form a conclusion. Give evidence to support each of your views or statements.
Evaluate critically	Review the information to decide the degree to which something is true, important or valuable. Then assess possible alternatives, taking into account their strengths and weaknesses if they were applied instead. Then give a precise and detailed account to explain your opinion.
Summarise	Identify/review the main, relevant factors and/or arguments so that these are explained in a clear and concise manner.
Examples: Assess ten features commonly found on a digital camera. Analyse your own ability to carry out effective research for an assignment.	

TOP TIP

Check that you understand exactly how you need to demonstrate each of the learning outcomes specified in the assignment.

Responding positively

Assignments enable you to demonstrate what you know and how you can apply it. You should respond positively to the challenge and give it your best shot. Being well organised and having confidence in your own abilities helps too, and this is covered in the next section.

Key points

- Read instructions carefully so that you don't make mistakes that can easily be avoided, such as only doing part of the set task.
- Note the assignment deadline on your planner and any interim review dates. Schedule work around these dates to make the most of reviews with your tutor.
- Check your centre's policies relating to assignments, such as how to obtain an extension or query a final grade.
- Expect command words and/or the complexity of a task to be different at higher grades, because you have to demonstrate higher-level skills.

TOP TIP

All your assignments will relate to topics you have covered and work you have done in class. They're not meant to be a test to catch you out.

Action points

1 Check your ability to differentiate between different types of command words by doing this activity.
   a) Prepare a brief description of your usual lifestyle (pass level).
   b) Describe and justify your current lifestyle (merit level).
   c) Critically evaluate your current lifestyle (distinction level).

It would be a good idea to check that your answer is accurate and appropriate by showing it to your tutor at your next tutorial.

TOP TIP

When presenting evidence for an assessment, think about the person who will be looking through it. Plan your 'pitch' well and make it easy for the assessor to match your evidence against the grading criteria.

Sample assignment

Note about assignments

All learners are different and will approach their assignment in different ways.
The sample assignment that follows shows how one learner answered a brief to achieve pass, merit and distinction level criteria. The learner work whose just one way in which grading criteria can be evidenced. There are no standard or set answers. If you produce the required evidence for each task then you will achieve the grading criteria covered by the assignment.

Front sheet

Pay close attention to the grading criteria for the assignment. These are the criteria the assessor will refer to when marking the work. Make sure you understand what is required for the higher grades.

It is important that you add your name to the assignment when you are given it.

Take note of the completion date. This is an important deadline. You should also make sure you are aware of your school or colleges policy on late completion of work.

Complete this box before you hand any work in. It will provide a record that you submitted your work on time.

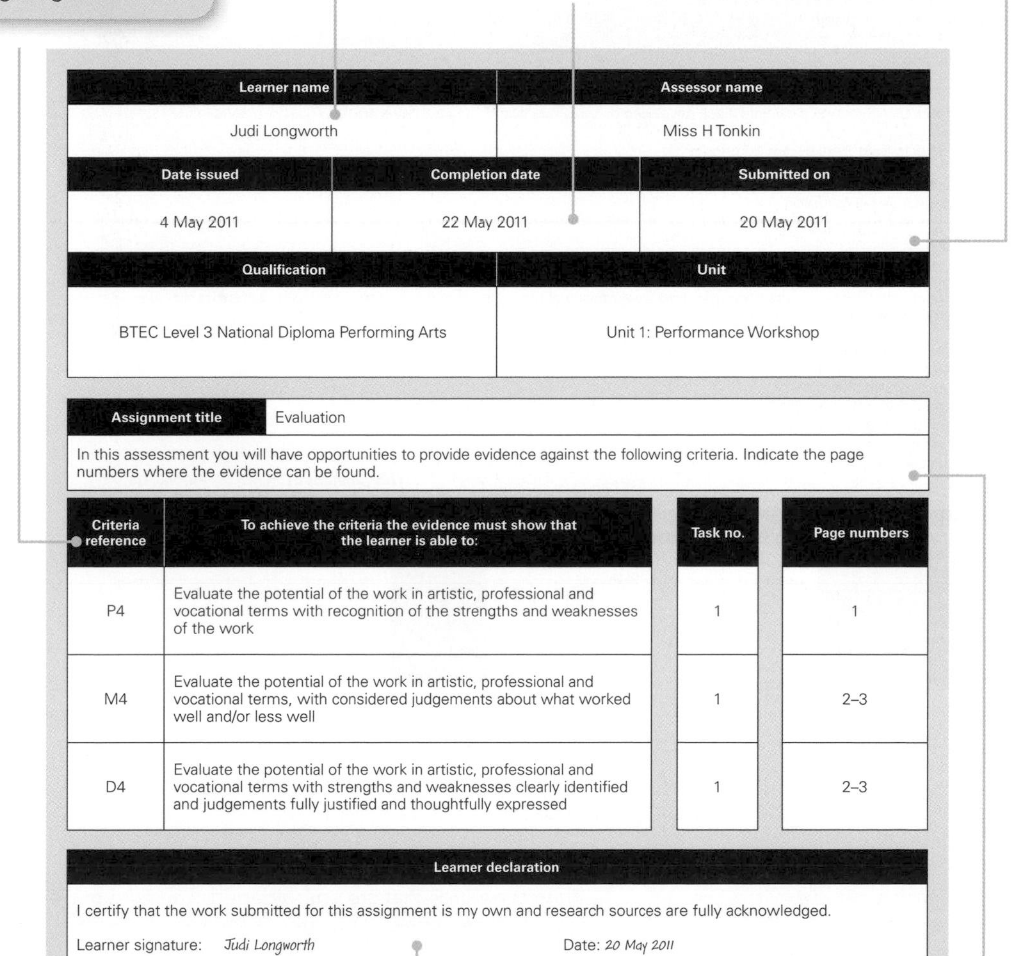

Learner name	Assessor name
Judi Longworth	Miss H Tonkin

Date issued	Completion date	Submitted on
4 May 2011	22 May 2011	20 May 2011

Qualification	Unit
BTEC Level 3 National Diploma Performing Arts	Unit 1: Performance Workshop

Assignment title Evaluation

In this assessment you will have opportunities to provide evidence against the following criteria. Indicate the page numbers where the evidence can be found.

Criteria reference	To achieve the criteria the evidence must show that the learner is able to:	Task no.	Page numbers
P4	Evaluate the potential of the work in artistic, professional and vocational terms with recognition of the strengths and weaknesses of the work	1	1
M4	Evaluate the potential of the work in artistic, professional and vocational terms, with considered judgements about what worked well and/or less well	1	2–3
D4	Evaluate the potential of the work in artistic, professional and vocational terms with strengths and weaknesses clearly identified and judgements fully justified and thoughtfully expressed	1	2–3

Learner declaration

I certify that the work submitted for this assignment is my own and research sources are fully acknowledged.

Learner signature: *Judi Longworth* Date: *20 May 2011*

On completion of your assignment you will be asked to sign this declaration indicating that the work handed in is your own. Make sure you are aware of the rules regarding plagiarism and always reference passages from books and the internet properly.

If you assignment includes written work you should make sure your portfolio clearly shows where the work for each individual task can be found in your portfolio or folder.

Assignment brief

The scenario provides an overview of the tasks and their context. In this example it refers back to work completed earlier in the unit.

The assignment title gives you a taste of what you will be doing during this piece of work. In this example it is clear that this assignment will involve you in reviewing the work completed in this unit.

Unit	Unit 1: Performance Workshop
Qualification	BTEC Level 3 National Diploma in Performing Arts/Production Arts
Start date	4 May 2011
Deadline date	22 May 2011
Assessor	H Tonkin

Assignment title	Evaluation

The purpose of this assignment is to:
allow learners to evaluate the workshop process in light of performance

Scenario
The work undertaken during this unit has included two workshop performances:

- *Precious Memories*, a devised piece developed by the group from a range of news articles about dementia in the elderly
- Extracts from *Road* by Jim Cartwright.

This assignment requires you to choose one of these workshop performances and evaluate its potential for development into a full-scale production.

Task 1

Choose one of the workshop performances produced during this unit. For the chosen piece you should produce a written evaluation that considers **the strengths and weaknesses** of the work we produced and assesses its **potential for development** into a full-scale production.

Your evaluation should include discussion of:
- the effectiveness of creative process
- working relationships
- use of performance skills
- clarity of interpretation
- time management
- audience response to the work.

This provides evidence for P4, M4, D4

This brief has been verified as being fit for purpose			
Assessor	Miss H Tonkin		
Signature	*Holly Tonkin*	Date	*14 April 2011*
Internal verifier	Mrs J Laski		
Signature	*Jade Laski*	Date	*14 April 2011*

The task is set out in a way that makes it easy to understand using bold print and bullet points.

Note the words that are emboldened. This is to make sure that the learner understands the key elements of the task i.e. the evaluation of 'strengths and weaknesses' and 'potential for development'. Both of these must be discussed for a successful outcome.

Sample learner work

The learner begins her evaluation with a clear introduction which sets out what she intends to cover in the piece.

The learner uses the bullet points from the task as headings ensuring that all the important points are covered.

Sample learner work: page 1

Workshop review

Introduction

I enjoyed preparing for both workshop productions. The scenes from 'Road' were interesting to work on but the piece I got the most out of was 'Precious Memories' – the piece we put together ourselves using information that we gathered together from the internet, newspaper articles, etc. Care of the elderly is an important subject and I have learnt so much about how dementia affects older people and how difficult it makes the lives of their families and neighbours.

The creative process

Strengths:

- the time spent working on the character of Bess, making her real
- leaving the ending 'open' for the audience to decide.

Weaknesses:

- not being able to let go of what was not working.

Naomi and I both worked on developing the character of Bess, who is the central character in 'Precious Memories'. She has Alzheimer's disease. We began by doing some research on dementia using the Alzheimer's Society and Age Concern websites. This research also took us to other sites that described elder abuse, which is when old people are bullied by people who are supposed to be looking after them. I found this quite upsetting.

It is very easy for young people like myself to forget that people like Bess were once teenagers with their whole lives ahead of them, so we wanted to make sure the character of Bess had a past. We needed to know more about her than that she was just a confused old lady. We decided how old she was and made a timeline for her – marking the personal events in her life like important birthdays, when she got married, when she had her son, when her husband died, etc. We then added important historical events to the timeline.

We also decided early on that we would not actually see Bess as an old lady on stage. At first I thought this was not a good idea and got a bit annoyed because we had done so much work in building her character. The decision was made partly because we didn't want to spoil the piece by having someone who was obviously young playing the part. In the end, I think it worked and the research we did on her character was still very important for Naomi who played her as a young girl. It also helped the other characters in how they reacted to her. In the end, I think it was good to see her only in flashback as she was then the same age as the kids in the street who were either bullying her or trying to help her. It was like she became invisible when she got old. (My mum says that happens when you get older!)

The story of what happened to Bess developed over about four lessons. We spent a long time thinking about an ending. We began with the idea of her being taken into hospital because she was run over. We spent ages working on the scene then decided it was not working. We should have changed our minds earlier but we didn't want to feel we had wasted the time. In the end, we decided to end with a question rather than an answer and that it should be left to the audience to decide what would happen to Bess. There were eventually three possible solutions, and each had good points and bad points.

Note how the learner uses one of the key statements from the tasks 'strengths and weaknesses' through the evaluation.

Here is an example of the learner making considered judgements about what went less well (M4)

Sample learner work: page 2

Working relationships

Strengths:
- use of company meetings.

Weaknesses:
- poor attendance from some people
- people letting friendships get in the way of the work.

I think we worked very well together. I really liked the idea that we were a theatre company as it helped us to concentrate on what we had to do.

We began each week with a company meeting. This was very good as we could look at what needed to be done next and make decisions about how we would do it. We took turns in running the meeting and this was usually okay except some people then gave the best jobs to their friends. When we began to rehearse it was sometimes difficult when people were off because we couldn't work on scenes they were in. There were also times when people began to argue and that was very unhelpful as it meant we couldn't get on.

Performance skills

Strengths:
- use of movement and vocal skills in Scenes 1–4.

Weaknesses:
- being able to show how the character has changed in Scene 6.

My character was Connie and she had to go through a change during the performance. She began as a typical bully, full of herself and very brash. I worked hard on my movement skills to get the body language and the voice just right. I also had to be careful not to go over the top and make her too much like Lauren or Vicky Pollard. In the last scene she realises just how dreadful she has been and this was more difficult in a way. She doesn't have much to say so I had to work hard on my facial expressions and gesture to get her feelings across.

Clarity of interpretation

Strengths:
- getting the message across.

Weaknesses:
- flashback monologues.

I think everyone in the group performed very well. We got the message across to the audience and during the last scene when the kids couldn't find Bess you could tell that the audience were really upset. At the beginning of the play some of the audience said they were a bit confused about the flashback monologues. They were not sure who Naomi was supposed to be.

Time management

Strengths:
- we met our deadlines.

Weaknesses:
- final week of rehearsals too rushed.

I think we made good use of the time we had. It took about a term to get the workshop ready using two lessons a week. We did waste some time in rehearsals which led to the last week being a bit rushed but on the whole we achieved what we set out to do.

Here the learner makes a considered judgement about something that went well (M4).

Here the learner covered the other key element of the task 'potential for future development'.

Sample learner work: page 3

Further development

Strengths:

- important issue for young people
- still things about Bess's story that could be explored.

Weaknesses:

- use of flashbacks could cause problems.

I think this workshop could and should be developed into a full-length play for young people. It is a very important topic. People of my age don't really understand what it is like to be old or what it is like to have to look after someone who is becoming confused. The workshop went down well with the audience and the feedback we got was very good. Some people said that it really made them think about old people living near to them.

The workshop only lasted 45 minutes and a complete performance would need to be at least twice that long. This means we would have to create more scenes. The bits of the play that could be developed are the scenes with Bess's son. We talked at first about there being a daughter as well. This would introduce more conflict into the piece as the daughter could have different views about what should happen to Bess. The character of the social worker could also be developed and we would actually be able to see the scene where there is a case conference rather than just hearing about it.

If the piece was developed we would also need to think hard about our use of flashbacks. We would need to make sure that members of the audience don't get lost. We could have proper scenes with characters from Bess's past rather than just monologues. If people are dressed in old-fashioned clothes, that might help.

This table shows the learner's achievement in this assignment. The 'Y' stands for 'yes' and shows criteria that have been successfully achieved, in this example P4 and M4. The 'N' stands for 'no' and indicates that the learner has not yet achieved D4.

Qualification	BTEC Level 3 National Diploma Performing Arts	Year	2010–2011
Unit number and title	Unit 1: Performance Workshop	Learner name	Judi Longworth

Grading criteria	Achieved?
P4 evaluate the potential of the work in artistic, professional and vocational terms with recognition of the strengths and weaknesses of the work.	Y
M4 evaluate the potential of the work in artistic, professional and vocational terms, with considered judgements about what worked well and/or less well.	Y
D4 evaluate the potential of the work in artistic, professional and vocational terms with strengths and weaknesses clearly identified and judgements fully justified and thoughtfully expressed.	N

Learner feedback

I found the evaluation a bit difficult to write although the headings we were given did help. I don't usually do well when I have to do written work so I am pleased with the grade I have been given.

Assessor feedback

Your report discusses the work in artistic, professional and vocational terms. You have produced an evaluation of the potential of the work making some clear and considered judgements about what worked well and less well. You have also made some thoughtful suggestions about how the work could be developed into a full-scale performance. For this, you have been awarded M4.

Action plan

To work towards achieving D4 you need to make closer reference to specific examples from the work when talking about strengths and weaknesses of the work. You should also discuss audience responses to the work.

Assessor signature	Holly Tonkin	Date	22 May 2011
Learner signature	Judi Longworth	Date	1st June 2011

The assessor has provided actions points for improvement. As this is a written assignment the learner may be allowed to redraft sections of the evaluation taking these actions into account.

Step Seven: Work productively as a member of a group

Case study: Working as a member of a group

Many people who earn a living in the performing arts work as part of performance and/or production company. A touring theatre company, for example, will employ performers and production staff, all of whom must work as a team to create the pieces of theatre that the company produces.

During many of the projects you will complete on your BTEC National in Performing Arts you will also be required to work as part of a performance/production company.

Learners at a college in the northwest were asked by their tutor to formalise their work as a company and the responsibilities of company members.

They did this by doing the following.

- They drew up a short list of aims and objectives to form the basis of an artistic policy for their company. For example, they decided that one of the company's aims was to create work to both inform and entertain their audiences.
- They agreed a name for their company and designed a company logo for use on all advertising materials for the shows they produced.
- They drew a list of ground rules setting out what was expected of company members. This included rules about timekeeping, respecting other company members and preparing fully for rehearsals and performances.
- They drew up a list of rehearsal room rules to ensure their time was used productively. These rules included not eating or using mobile phones and sitting quietly when not involved in the scene being rehearsed.
- They drafted a company 'contract' stating the responsibilities of its members.
- When the contract had been agreed, they typed it up and provided a copy for each company member to sign.
- The group also attached a large copy of the contract to the wall of their workspace.

Reflection points

- Do you think these activities will help the learners work together as a company during their projects?
- Why is teamwork so vital to those studying on a performing arts programme?
- Think about team situations you have been in. Do you usually speak out more than you observe and listen? Or vice versa?
- Think about why a team needs a leader. How would you choose a team leader?

In your private life, you can choose your own friends, at work you are paid to work alongside many people; whether you like them or not.

This applies at school or college too. Hopefully, by now, you've outgrown wanting to only work with your best friends on every project.

You may not be keen on everyone in your team, but you should still be pleasant and co-operative. This may be harder if you are working with a partner than in a large group.

Sometimes you may be the group leader. This may inspire you, or fill you with dread. You won't be expected to develop team-leader skills overnight, but it helps if you know the basics.

First, you should understand how groups and teams work and why good teamwork is considered vital by employers.

Working in groups and teams

If you have a full- or part-time job, you already belong to a working group, or team. At school or college your class is an example of a working group.

All working groups have some common characteristics:

- doing the same type of work – though in the workplace you probably have different roles or responsibilities
- a group leader or supervisor
- a reason for working together, such as studying for the same qualification or tackling an area of work too large for someone to do alone
- group members are dependent on each other in some way; at work you may have to cover someone's workload if they are absent
- group members concentrate on their individual achievements and success.

A team is different. As a team member you have a specific objective to achieve **together** – and this is more important than the goals of individual team members.

TOP TIP

Understanding how groups and teams function will help you be a better team worker and a better team leader.

These are the characteristics of a team.

- Team members have a team goal which is more important than any personal goals.
- Team members have complementary skills so that the team can achieve more than individuals working alone could achieve.
- Work is allocated to play to each person's strengths and talents.
- The team members give each other encouragement and support.
- There is collective responsibility for achieving the goal.

A good team leader acts as facilitator and motivator, and gives practical support and guidance.

Working in a team has many benefits. Team members can learn from each other and combine their skills to do a better job more quickly. Working with other people is often more enjoyable than working alone, too. Many industries rely heavily on efficient group working, from IT teams to health workers and the emergency services.

TOP TIP

Focusing on the task rather than on personalities is the first step in learning to work with different people, whose views may not match your own.

There are many benefits to be gained from working as a team.

Being a good team member

Everyone wants team members who are talented, positive, cheerful and full of energy. These are the key areas to focus on if you wish to be a good team member.

- **Your social skills.** This includes being courteous, treating other people as you wish to be treated, saying 'please' when you want something and thanking people who do you a favour.
- **Your temperament**. Expect people to have different views and opinions from you and don't take offence if someone disagrees with you. If you lose your temper easily, learn to walk away before you say something you may regret.
- **Your communication skills.** This includes talking and listening!

  Practise saying what you mean clearly, accurately and succinctly. Be prepared to give good reasons to justify your arguments and ideas.

  Allow people to finish what they're saying, without interruption, before you talk. Never shout people down. Think before you speak so that you don't upset people with tactless remarks. If you inadvertently do so, apologise.
- **Your commitment.** Always keep your promises and never let anyone down when they are depending upon you. Always do your fair share of the work, even if you don't agree with all the decisions made by your team. Tell people promptly if you are having problems so there is time to solve them. Be loyal to your team when you're talking to other people.

Being the team leader

It can be difficult to strike a balance between 'leading' the team and working with friends. You need to inspire and motivate your team without being bossy or critical.

Important points to remember about being a team leader

- Lead by example. Stay pleasant, consistent and control your temper, even under pressure.
- Everyone is different. Your ways of working may not always be the best.
- Be prepared to listen and contribute positively to a discussion.
- Encourage quieter team members to join in discussions by asking for their views.
- Be prepared to do whatever you ask other people to do.
- Note down what you say you will do, so that you don't forget.
- Discuss alternatives with people rather than giving orders.
- Be sensitive to other people's feelings. They may have personal problems or issues that affect their behaviour.
- Learn the art of persuasion.
- Act as peacemaker. Help people reach a compromise when necessary.
- Give team members the credit for their hard work or good ideas.
- Admit your mistakes. Look for a positive solution and think about what can be learned for the future, rather than making excuses.
- Praise and encourage team members who are working hard.
- Make criticisms constructively, and in private.
- Be assertive (put forward your point of view firmly) rather than aggressive (attacking other people to defend yourself.)

Some notes of caution about being a team leader

- Try to look pleasant and don't glare at people who interrupt you unexpectedly.
- Never talk about team members behind their backs.
- Don't gossip, exaggerate to make a point, spread rumours, speculate or tell lies.
- Don't expect to get your own way all the time – all good leaders back down on occasion.
- Never criticise any colleagues in front of other people. Speak to them in private and keep it constructive.

TOP TIP

Excellent ideas often come from quiet team members. Encourage everyone to make suggestions so that you don't overlook any valuable contributions.

Key points

- There are many benefits of working in a group or as a team. These include mutual support, companionship and the exchange of ideas.
- You will be expected to work co-operatively with other people at work, and during many course assignments.
- It isn't easy learning to be a team leader. Team leaders should be fair, consistent and pleasant to work with, as well as loyal and sensitive to the needs of team members.

Action points

1 Identify the role of teamwork in your area of study. Identify the team's goal and any factors you think will contribute towards its success.

2 Decide how you would handle each of the following difficult situations if you were the team leader. If you can, discuss your ideas with a friend in your class.

a) The team needs to borrow a college video camera to record an event being held tonight. Your tutor tells you that the one you reserved last week is not working and the rest are out on loan.

b) A member of your team has personal problems so you have given him less work to do. Now you've been accused of having favourites.

c) A team member is constantly letting everyone down because of poor work and non-attendance at group meetings.

d) Two team members have disagreed about how to do a task. You're not bothered how they do it as long as it gets done properly, and by the deadline.

e) A team member becomes very aggressive whenever she is challenged in any way – no matter how mildly.

3 Identify someone who has inspired you because they've been an excellent leader. This could be someone you've met, a fictional character or a famous person. Note down what it is about them that impressed you.

Activity: Teamwork during rehearsals

Rehearsals are central to the preparation of any type of performance work. It is when ideas are tried out, scenes are run through, and dance routines are learned and practised. Well-organised and carefully run rehearsals are essential to the success of any performing arts production and it is vital that the group works as a team to ensure the time is used productively.

Taking part in a rehearsal is hard work. There will be times when you are actively involved in the process and times when you will need to sit quietly and observe. It is vital that concentration and focus are maintained throughout. Behaviour such as chatting or texting will cause you to lose focus and is distracting for those directly involved in a scene or routine.

Come up with **3 Golden Rules** for good behaviour in the rehearsal room.

1.
2.
3.

Rehearsals are often a time for taking risks and trying things out. It is therefore essential that there is a supportive atmosphere in the rehearsal room. Group members must feel comfortable with each other. They must feel that they suggest and can try out ideas without being laughed at or ridiculed.

Come up with **3 Golden Rules** for supporting other members of the group during rehearsals.

1.
2.
3.

Activity: Teamwork during production tasks

If you are studying on the production pathway, teamwork will also be an important factor in the work you do. The design, technical and production staff working on a performing arts event need to work as a well-organised group before, during and after each show.

Good communication is vital to ensure a project progresses as it should. When working with others it is important that you express yourself clearly, while also taking into consideration the views of others.

For example: Learners at a college are discussing a number of different ideas for the design of a set for 'A Midsummer Night's Dream'. While looking at the design ideas put forward by one learner another member of the group says: **'This is rubbish. It will never work.'**

What might the effect of this comment be on:

1 the learner whose design ideas were being discussed?
2 other learners in the group?

When you think an idea is not right for a project it is important that you say so. You must, however, try to provide constructive feedback rather than just saying that something is no good!

For example, another way of communicating concern over the idea might have been to say: **'This looks good, but I'm not sure how it will work in practice as it seems very complicated.'** Why might this response be more appropriate?

Consider the statements below and suggest a more appropriate comment in each case.

What was said	How it might have been said
'This is practically identical to the last design you came up with. You haven't even tried.'	
'I'm just sick of his ideas always being the ones that get chosen for the production. I don't know why the rest of us bother.'	
'Why can't you shut up and let someone else speak?'	
'This is the first time you've turned up in weeks. I don't see why we should listen to you.'	

Step Eight: Understand how to research and analyse information

Case study: Finding and analysing information about jobs

You will undertake a lot of practical work as part of your BTEC National in Performing Arts. Some of the work set will, however, require traditional research tasks.

Like the learners below you may be required undertake research for many different reasons, just as people do when working in the performing arts industry.

- Hari is a design student who is heading up the costume design team for a production of 'A Midsummer Night's Dream', which is to be set in the 1920s. He begins by undertaking research into the clothing of the time looking at examples from the working, middle and upper classes using both the Internet and books in his college library as a starting point.
- Bella is a dance student who is undertaking an investigation into the work of three major choreographers of the 20th century for a dance appreciation presentation. She starts by searching for videos showing the choreographers' work.
- Genna is an acting student playing a World War 2 evacuee in a devised piece of theatre. She undertakes some primary research to help inform the development of her character by talking to a number of elderly people who were themselves evacuated during the war.
- Rudi is a production student who is working in the role of lighting designer for a musical theatre production. He needs to find out about companies that hire out lighting and other specialist stage equipment in his local area.

Reflection points

- How do you think research skills might be used on your chosen pathway?
- What experience do you have of research activities from previous courses you have undertaken?
- Think about how you have researched information in the past. Were your techniques effective? How could you make improvements?

As a BTEC Level 3 National learner, you often have to find information for yourself. This skill will be invaluable in your working life, and if you continue your studies at higher education (HE) level. Sometimes the information will give you a better understanding of a topic, at other times you will research to obtain information for a project or assignment. Sometimes you may be so interested in something that you want to find out more without being told to do so!

Whatever your reason, and no matter where your information can be found, there is a good and not so good way to go about the task. This section will help if you can't find what you want, or find too much, or drift aimlessly around a library, or watch a demonstration and don't know what to ask afterwards.

Types of information

There are many types of information and many different sources. Depending on the task, these are the sources you may need to consult:

- **Verbal information.** This includes talking to friends, colleagues at work, members of your family, listening to experts explain what they do, interviewing people, talking to sales reps at an exhibition or customers about a product.
- **Printed information**. This includes information printed in newspapers, journals, magazines, books, posters, workshop manuals, leaflets and catalogues. The type of magazine or newspaper you read may have its own slant on the information, which you may have to take into account (see page 57).
- **Written information**. This includes course notes and handouts, reports and other documents in the workplace. If you want to use written information from work, you must check this is allowed, and that it doesn't contain confidential material such as financial information or staff names and addresses.
- **Graphical information.** This includes illustrations, pictures, cartoons, line drawings, graphs and photographs. Graphics can make something clearer than words alone. For example, a satnav instruction book might contain illustrations to show different procedures.
- **Electronic information.** This includes information from electronic sources such as DVDs, CD-ROMs, searchable databases, websites, podcasts, webinars (**seminars** online), emails and text messages. The huge amount of information available online is both a help and a hindrance. You can find information quickly, but the source may be unreliable, out-of-date, inaccurate or inappropriate (see page 56.)

TOP TIP

Too much information is as bad as too little, because it's overwhelming. The trick is to find good quality, relevant information and know when to call a halt to your search.

TOP TIP

Consider all appropriate sources and don't just rely on information found online.

Finding what you need

Spend a few minutes planning what to do before you start looking for information. This can save a lot of time later on.

The following steps will help you to do this.

1. Make sure you understand exactly what it is you need to know so that you don't waste time looking for the wrong thing.
2. Clarify your objectives to narrow down your search. Think about why the information is wanted and how much detail you need. For example, learners studying BTEC Nationals in Engineering and Performing Arts may both be researching 'noise' for their projects but they are likely to need different types of information and use it in different ways.
3. Identify your sources and check you know how to use them. You need to choose sources that are most likely to provide information relevant to your objectives. For example, an Engineering learner might find information on noise emissions in industry journals and by checking out specialist websites.
4. Plan and schedule your research. Theoretically, you could research information forever. Knowing when to call a halt takes skill. Write a schedule that states when you must stop looking and start sorting the information.
5. Store your information safely in a labelled folder. This folder should include printouts or photocopies of articles, notes about events you have attended or observed, photographs you've taken or sketches you've drawn. Divide your information under topic headings to make it easier to find. When you're ready to start work, re-read your assignment brief and select the items that are most closely related to the task you are doing.

TOP TIP

Allocate time for research as part of your assignment task. Take into account any interim deadlines as well as the final deadline for completing the work.

Primary and secondary research, and the law of copyright

There are two ways to research information. One is known as primary research, the other is secondary research.

Primary research

Primary research involves finding new information about an issue or topic. This might include finding out people's views about a product or interviewing an expert. When carrying out interviews, you will need to design a survey or questionnaire. Your primary research might also include observing or experiencing something for yourself, and recording your feelings and observations.

Secondary research

Secondary research involves accessing information that already exists in books, files, newspapers or on CD-ROMs, computer databases or the internet, and assessing it against your objectives.

This information has been prepared by other people and is available to anyone. You can quote from an original work provided you acknowledge the source of your information. You should put this acknowledgement in your text or in the bibliography to your text; do not claim it as your own research. You must include the author's name, year of publication, the title and publisher, or the web address if it is an online article. You should practise listing the sources of articles so that you feel confident writing a bibliography. Use the guidance sheet issued by your centre to help you. This will illustrate the style your centre recommends.

The trick with research is to choose the best technique to achieve your objectives and this may mean using a mix of methods and resources. For example, if you have to comment on an industry event you might go to it, make notes, interview people attending, observe the event (perhaps take a video camera), and read any newspaper reports or online comments.

TOP TIP

Always make sure you make a note of where you get information from (your source). Keep it safely as it can be very difficult later on to work out where it came from!

People as a source of information

If you want to get the most out of interviewing someone, or several people, you need to prepare carefully in advance.

The following points give some general advice about getting the most out of face-to-face interviews.

- Make sure you know what questions to ask to get the information you need.
- Explain why you want the information.
- Don't expect to be told confidential or sensitive information.
- Write clear notes so that you remember who told you what, and when. (See also page 58.)
- Note the contact details of the person you are interviewing and ask whether they mind if you contact them again should you think of anything later or need to clarify your notes.
- Thank them for their help.

If you want to ask a lot of people for their opinion you may want to conduct a survey. You will need to design a questionnaire and analyse the results. This will be easier if you ask for **quantitative** responses – for example yes/no, true/false or ratings on a five-point scale – rather than opinions.

- Give careful thought to your representative sample (people whose opinions are relevant to the topic.)
- Decide how many people to survey so that the results mean something.
- Keep the survey relatively short.
- Thank people who complete it.
- Analyse the results, and write up your conclusions promptly.

TOP TIP

Test your questionnaire on volunteers before you 'go live' to check that there are no mistakes and the questions are easy to understand. Make any amendments before you conduct your 'real' survey.

Asking someone who knows a lot about a topic can be informative.

Avoiding pitfalls

Wikipedia is a good online source that covers many topics, and often in some depth. It is popular and free. However, it has an open-content policy, which means that anyone can contribute to and edit entries. People may post information, whether it is correct or not. Wikipedia is moving towards greater checks on entries, but it is still sensible to check out information you find on this site somewhere else.

Apart from inaccuracy, you may find other problems with information you obtain through research, especially material found online.

- **Out-of-date material.** Check the date of everything and keep only the latest version of books, newspapers or magazines. Yesterday's news may be of little use if you are researching something topical.
- **Irrelevant details.** Often, only part of an article will be relevant to your search. For example, if you are forecasting future trends in an area of work, you do not need information about its history or related problems. When learners are struggling, they sometimes 'pad out' answers with irrelevant information. If you've researched properly you can avoid this by having enough relevant information for your purposes.

- **Invalid assumptions.** This means someone has jumped to the wrong conclusion and made 2 + 2 = 5. You might do this if you see two friends chatting and think they are talking about you – whether they are or not! You can avoid problems in this area by double-checking your ideas and getting evidence to support them.
- **Bias.** This is when people hold strong views about a topic, or let their emotions or prejudices affect their judgement. An obvious example is asking a keen football fan for an objective evaluation of their team's performance!
- **Vested interests.** People may argue in a certain way because it's in their own interests to do so. For example, when the Government said Home Information Packs must be prepared for all properties being sold, the Association of Home Information Pack Providers was in favour because it trains the people who prepare the packs. The National Association of Estate Agents and Royal Institution of Chartered Surveyors were not because they thought they would lose business if people were put off selling their houses.

TOP TIP

Don't discard information that is affected by bias or vested interests. Just make it clear you know about the problem and have taken it into account.

Reading for a purpose

You may enjoy reading or you may find it tedious or difficult. If so, it helps to know that there are different ways to read, depending on what you're doing. For example, you wouldn't look for a programme in a TV guide in the same way that you would check an assignment for mistakes. You can save time and find information more easily if you use the best method of reading to suit your purpose. The following are some examples of ways of reading.

- **Skim reading** is used to check new information and get a general overview.
  To skim a book chapter read the first and last paragraphs, the headings, subheadings and illustrations. It also helps to read the first sentence of each paragraph.

TOP TIP

News articles are written with the key points at the beginning, so concentrate on the first paragraph or two. Feature articles have a general introduction and important information is contained in the main text.

- **Scanning** is used to see whether an article contains something you need – such as key words, dates or technical terms.
  Focus on capital or initial letters for a name, and figures for a date. Technical terms may be in bold or italics.
- **Light reading** is usually done for pleasure when you are relaxed, for example, reading a magazine article. You may not remember many facts afterwards, so this sort of reading isn't suitable for learning something or assessing its value.
- **Word-by-word reading (proofreading)** is important so that you don't miss anything, such as the dosage instructions for a strong medicine. You should proofread assignments before you submit them.
- **Reading for study (active reading)** means being actively involved so that you understand the information. It is rare to be naturally good at this, so you might have to work to develop this skill.

Developing critical and analytical skills

Developing critical and analytical skills involves looking at information for any flaws in the arguments. These skills are important when you progress to work or higher education (HE), so it's useful to practise them now on your BTEC Level 3 National course.

A useful technique for understanding, analysing, evaluating and remembering what you are reading is **SQ4R**.

SQ4R is an effective method. It consists of six steps.

1 Survey first, to get a general impression. Scan the information to see what it is about, when it was written and by whom. The source, and the reason it was written, may be important. Most newspapers, for example, have their own 'slant' that affects how information is presented.

2 Question your aims for reading this material. What are you hoping to find? What questions are you expecting it to answer?

3 Read the information three or four times. The first time, aim to get a general idea of the content. Use a dictionary to look up any new words. Then read more carefully to really understand what the writer means.

4 Respond by thinking critically about the information and how it relates to the topic you are studying. Does it answer your queries partially, fully or not at all? What information is factual and what is based on opinion? Is there evidence to support these opinions? Is there a reason why the author has taken this standpoint? Do you agree with it? How does it link to other information you have read? What is the opposite argument and is there any evidence to support this? Overall, how useful is this information?

5 Record the information by noting the key points. Use this to refresh your memory, if necessary, rather than re-reading the article.

6 Review your notes against the original to check you have included all important points. If you are also preparing a presentation, reviewing your notes will help you to remember key points more easily.

TOP TIP

SQ4R is just one method of reading for study. Research others and adapt them to suit your own style.

Taking good notes

There are many occasions when you need to take notes, such as when a visiting speaker is talking to your class. There's no point taking notes unless you write them in a way that will allow you to use them later.

Note-taking is a personal activity. Some people prefer to make diagrammatical sketches with key points in boxes linked by arrows; others prefer to write a series of bullet points. You will develop your own style, but the following hints and tips might help you at the start.

- Use A4 lined paper, rather than a notebook, so that you have more space and don't need to turn over so often.
- When you're reading for study, make sure you have a dictionary, pen, notepad and highlighter to hand.
- Leave a wide margin to record your own comments or queries.
- Put a heading at the top, such as the speaker's name and topic, as well as the date.
- If you are making notes from a book or an article, remember SQ4R and read it several times first. Your notes will only be effective if you understand the information.
- Don't write in complete sentences – it takes too long.
- Leave spaces for later additions or corrections.
- Use headings to keep your notes clear and well organised.
- Only write down relevant information, including key words and phrases.

- Highlight, underline or use capitals for essential points.
- Never copy chunks of text – always use your own words.
- Clearly identify quotations, and record your sources, so that you can cite them in your work. (Note the author's name, title, publisher, date and place of publication and the page number.)

TOP TIP

Make sure your information is accurate, up-to-date, relevant and valid. Be aware of bias, and don't confuse fact with opinion.

Key points

- Useful information may be verbal, printed, written, graphical or electronic.
- Effective research means knowing exactly what you are trying to find and where to look. Know how reference media are stored in your library and how to search online. Store important information carefully.
- Primary research is original data you obtain yourself. Secondary research is information prepared by someone else. If you use this, you must quote your sources in a bibliography.
- You can search for information by skimming and scanning, and read in different ways. Reading for study means actively involving yourself with the text, questioning what you are reading and making notes to help your own understanding.
- Read widely around a topic to get different viewpoints. Don't accept everything you read as correct. Think about how it fits with other information you have obtained.
- Taking notes is a personal skill that takes time to develop. Start by using A4 lined pages with a margin, set out your notes clearly and label them. Only record essential information.

Action points

- Working with a friend, look back at the sources of information listed on page 54. For each type, identify examples of information relevant to your course that you could obtain from each source. See how many you can list under each type.
- Check your ability to find the information you need by answering each of the questions in **Activity: Finding information** on the next page. For any questions you get wrong, your first research task is to find out the correct answers as quickly as you can.
- To check your ability to skim and scan information, improve your ability to differentiate fact from opinion, summarise text and much more, go to page 86 for information on how to access useful websites.
- Check your ability to sort fact from opinion and spot vested interests by completing **Activity: Let's give you a tip...** on page 62. Check your ideas with the answers on page 85.

TOP TIP

Make a note of any information that you are struggling to understand so that you can discuss it with your tutor.

Activity: Finding information

Answer the following questions about finding information.

a) Four types of information that are available from the library in your centre, besides books, are:

1

2

3

4

b) When I visit the library, the way to check if a book I want is available is:

c) The difference between borrowing a book on short-term loan and on long-term loan is:

Short-term loan:

Long-term loan:

d) The journals that are stocked by the library that are relevant to my course include:

e) Useful information on the intranet at my centre includes:

f) Searchable databases and online magazines I can access include:

g) The quickest way to check if a book or journal contains the type of information I need is to:

h) The difference between a search engine, a portal, a directory site and a forum is:

i) Bookmarking useful websites means:

j) In addition to suggesting websites, Google can also provide the following types of information:

k) Specialist websites which provide useful information related to my course include:

l) Useful tips I would give to people starting on my course who need to find out information are:

Activity: Let's give you a tip...

In 2009, many businesses were struggling thanks to the credit crunch and falling consumer demand. Some, like Woolworths, closed down altogether. Others laid off staff, or announced wage cuts. Despite this, the Government approved recommendations by the Low Pay Commission to increase the minimum wage rate from October. Although the rise was only small, many unions, including Unison and Usdaw, agreed it was better than a freeze, which had been wanted by the British Chambers of Commerce and the British Retail Consortium.

The Government also announced new laws to stop restaurants and bars using tips to top up staff pay to the minimum level. *The Independent* newspaper claimed its 'fair tips, fair pay' campaign had won the day. It also reported that the British Hospitality Association was claiming this could result in up to 45,000 job losses. The Unite union also carried out a campaign and its General Secretary claimed the decision a triumph for the poorly paid. Not everyone agreed. Some thought there should be no tipping at all, as in Australia. Others said the Canadian system was best – wages are low but generous tips are left, and this motivates staff to give excellent service.

a) Look at the table below. In your view, which of the statements are facts and which are opinions? In each case, justify your view.

Statement	Fact or opinion?	Justification
i) Having a national minimum wage helps low-paid workers.		
ii) Over one million people will benefit from the minimum wage increase.		
iii) The new law on tips will stop restaurants paying below minimum wage rates.		
iv) Using the Australian system of no tips would be better.		
v) The Canadian system guarantees good service.		
vi) 45,000 job losses will occur in the hospitality industry.		

b) All newspapers have their own way of putting forward the news. Go to page 86 to find out how you can access a website which will help you to compare the way that news is reported in different newspapers.

Compare six different newspapers and make notes on:

i) the type of stories covered

ii) the way views are put forward.

Activity: How to go about your research

If you are completing a project that involves research it is a good idea to keep a research log that:

- lists the resources you used and the materials you looked at
- states when and where they were found and how one source led to another where relevant
- sums up very briefly what was learned from each resource.

Below is an example of a research log being used by Hari, who is investigating 1920s fashion for a costume design project.

Name: Hari Benton **Assignment: A Midsummer Night's Dream – Costumes**				
Source/ material	**When and where found**	**How found**	**Overview of information gathered**	**Comments**
'Fashion-Era' website	Internet	Search engine	Overview of the main trends and developments in 1920s fashion.	A good resource with useful sketches and photographs.
The Complete History of Fashion and Costume – Cosgrove, B. Facts on File Inc., 2001	College library	Catalogue search	Summary of the main trends and developments in 1920s fashion.	Chapter on 1920s fashion includes some good illustrations.
Interview with Keely Barratt, freelance costume designer	Interview on 12/11/09 at Keely's studio	Interview arranged after Keely's details were given to me by my tutor	Keely showed me designs she created for a similar production set in the 1920s. We discussed the main features of fashion for both men and women.	This was really useful. Keely was very helpful and answered all my questions.

Adapt Hari's log for use as a template when you undertake a task that involves research.

Step Nine: Make an effective presentation

Case study: Well-prepared presentations

Presenting and sharing work with other learners will be a regular activity on your BTEC National in Performing Arts, whether you are delivering a PowerPoint presentation about a drama practitioner you have researched or sharing a dance piece you have created.

Musical theatre students at Hall Road College have just undertaken their first assignment for the Variety Performance unit. The assignment required them to research different types of variety acts and venues and present the results of their investigations to the class using PowerPoint.

Many of the learners found this assignment to be challenging and said they felt nervous presenting their work to the class even though they were used to performing in front of each other.

Whenever you take part in a session like this try to put your fellow learners at ease.

If you are watching a presentation:

- Treat the presenter with respect by listening attentively.
- Remember that criticism should always be constructive. Don't simply say you didn't like something. Try to explain how it might have been improved.
- Try to find something good to say to balance out any negative comments.

If you are presenting work:

- Try not to take criticism personally. It is the work, not you as a person, that is being discussed.

Whether you are watching or presenting you should remember that you are not in competition with each other. Try to think of yourselves as critical friends who support one another.

Reflection points

- Why do you think learners found this activity more nerve-racking than singing or dancing in front of each other?
- Have you ever had to present information to a group of people? How did it make you feel?
- Thinking about a presentation you have given in the past, what were your strengths and weaknesses as a presenter? How could you make improvements for the future?

Making a presentation can be nerve-wracking. It involves several skills, including planning, preparation and communication. It tests your ability to work in a team, speak in public and use IT (normally PowerPoint.) You also have to stay calm under pressure. However, as it is excellent practice for your future, you can expect presentations to be a common method of assessing your performance.

TOP TIP

When giving a presentation, keep to time, get to the point and use your time well.

Good planning and preparation

Being well prepared, and rehearsing beforehand, helps your confidence and your presentation. The following points will help you to do this.

- If you're part of a team, find out everyone's strengths and weaknesses and divide work fairly taking these into account. Decide how long each person should speak, who should introduce the team and who will summarise at the end.
- Take into account your time-scale, resources and team skills. A simple, clear presentation is better – and safer – than a complicated one.
- If you're using PowerPoint, make slides more interesting by avoiding a series of bulleted lists and including artwork. Print PowerPoint notes for the audience. Use a fuller set of notes for yourself, as a prompt.
- Check the venue and time.
- Decide what to wear and check it's clean and presentable.
- Prepare, check and print your handouts.
- Decide, as a team, the order in which people will speak, bearing in mind the topic.
- Discuss possible questions and how to answer them.
- Rehearse beforehand to check your timings.

If you prepare properly you can really enjoy giving a presentation.

TOP TIP

Rehearsing properly allows you to speak fluently, just glancing at your notes to remind you of the next key point.

On the day, you can achieve a better performance if you:

- arrive in plenty of time
- calm your nerves by taking deep breaths before going in front of your audience
- introduce yourself clearly, and smile at the audience
- avoid reading from your screen or your notes
- explain what you are going to do – especially if giving a demonstration – do it and then review what you've done
- say you will deal with questions at the end of any demonstration
- answer questions honestly – don't exaggerate, guess or waffle
- respond positively to all feedback, which should be used to improve your performance next time.

TOP TIPS

Make sure you can be heard clearly by lifting your head and speaking a little more slowly and loudly than normal.

Key points

- When making a presentation, prepare well, don't be too ambitious and have several rehearsals.
- When giving a demonstration, explain first what you are going to do and that you will answer questions at the end.

Case study: Learner quotes about making presentations

Most people start off feeling uncomfortable about talking in front of a group of people, whether you know them or not. This is what some real learners have said about having to give presentations as part of their BTEC course.

"I actually feel more comfortable giving a presentation rather than having to write an essay. What I really enjoy about it is the fact that sometimes we have to prepare a presentation as a whole group. I like that we work together to find information and then we take turns presenting different points. The fact that I am not the only one out there and I am part of a supportive team makes it fun for me."

Gabriela, 16, BTEC Level 2 First in Performing Arts

"Although presentations are very stressful, when I present my work it helps to hang my ideas together and I find I can express what I want to say more clearly than when I write things down. Instant feedback is helpful and boosts my confidence for the next time."

Ethan, 19, BTEC Level 2 First in Creative Media Production

"I think presentations are useful but I find them difficult to deliver – relying heavily on my memory, which is very nerve-racking. We were told that presentation would be part of our assessment. I really worried about it and couldn't sleep the night before – stressing out about what I was going to say. I hated the first few minutes, but after that I was OK."

Will, 16, BTEC Level 2 First in Engineering

"I was very nervous about presenting to my class until I took part in the Young Enterprise scheme and had to present the results of our project to over 200 people including the mayor! After that presenting to my class mates didn't feel too nerve wracking at all."

Lizzy, 17, BTEC Level 2 First in Business

"I used to dread presentations on my course, but found that if I went through my notes again and again until I knew the presentation inside out, it made it much easier and the presentations generally went well."

Javinder, 17, BTEC Level 3 National in Construction

Activity: All right on the night?

Read the following account and answer the questions that follow. If possible, compare ideas with a friend in your class.

Gemma looked around in exasperation. The team were on the final rehearsal of their presentation and nothing was going right. Amaya seemed to think it was funny. 'Honestly, Gemma, why don't you just chill for a bit?' she suggested. 'You know what they say – a bad dress rehearsal means we'll do really well tomorrow!'

Gemma glared at her. 'Well, can I make a suggestion, too, Amaya,' she retorted. 'Why don't you just concentrate for a change? Sprawling around and dissolving into giggles every five minutes isn't helping either.'

She turned to Adam. 'And I thought you were going to build a simple model,' she said, 'not one that falls apart every time you touch it.'

Adam looked crest-fallen. 'But I wanted to show how it worked.'

'How it's supposed to work, you mean!' raged Gemma, all her worries and anxieties now coming to the fore. 'We'll look stupid if it ends up in bits on the floor tomorrow and Amaya just falls about laughing again.'

'And Imran,' continued Gemma, turning her sights on the last member of the team, 'why is it so difficult for you to count to three minutes? We've agreed over and over again we'll each talk for three minutes and every time you get carried away with the sound of your own voice and talk for twice as long. It just means we're going to overrun and get penalised. And stop trying to wriggle out of answering questions properly. For heaven's sake, if you don't know the answer, how hard is it just to say so?'

Silence fell. No-one looked at each other. Adam fiddled with his model and something else fell off. Amaya wanted to laugh but didn't dare.

Imran was sulking and vowed never to say anything ever again. 'You wait,' he thought. 'Tomorrow I'll race through my part in one minute flat. And then what are you going to do?'

1 Identify the strengths and weaknesses of each member of the presentation team.

Name	Strengths	Weaknesses
Gemma		
Amaya		
Adam		
Imran		

2 What have the team done right, so far, in getting ready for their presentation?

3 Why do you think they are having problems?

4 If you were Gemma's tutor, what advice would you give her at this point?

Activity: Approaches to presentations

How well will you cope with the presentations you will have to take part in on your BTEC Level 3 National In Performing Arts?

This quiz should get you thinking!

1 You have just finished your presentation on the importance of marketing in the performing arts. Someone in your class asks a question you don't know the answer to. What do you do?

a) Try to avoid the question by trying to change the subject.

b) Admit that you don't know the answer.

c) Make something up – they'll probably never realise.

2 A learner on your course is delivering a presentation on dance practitioners. He is obviously very nervous. What do you do?

a) Sink into your chair with embarrassment.

b) Look at him and smile in an encouraging way.

c) Try to think of a difficult question to ask at the end.

3 It is the day before an important presentation and you have forgotten to book a place in the computer suite. This means there is no way you'll get your PowerPoint finished in time. What do you do?

a) Pretend to be unwell.

b) Come clean, apologise, and try to get through the presentation anyway.

c) Blame someone else.

4 The class has been divided into groups and asked to come up with ideas for a devised piece of children's theatre. When the time comes to present and share ideas you find that the first group up has come up with a very similar idea to the one your group has chosen. What do you do?

a) Make an excuse and go to the loo when it's your group's turn.

b) Present your idea anyway.

c) Accuse the other group of stealing your idea.

5 You have been working as part of a group of four coming up with and developing ideas for costumes for *Les Miserables*. One member of your group has not been pulling her weight and as the presentation approaches you are worried that it will affect the group's performance. What do you do?

a) Cross your fingers and hope she doesn't turn up for the presentation.

b) Talk to the tutor and ask his/her advice.

c) Lose your temper with her and tell her not to bother turning up on the day.

How did you do?

Mostly a – You like to keep your head down and avoid difficult issues. This might be because you don't like to get into difficult situations but it will not be helpful when preparing, delivering or even watching presentations.

Mostly b – You are generally well organised and supportive of others. You should do well.

Mostly c – Although there are times when being firm with people is important you should always try to be fair. You will get more from your work if you try to be more supportive of others.

Step Ten: Maximise your opportunities and manage your problems

Case study: Managing your problems

Your time on your BTEC National will be full of both opportunities to help you get the best out of your course and problems that may threaten your progress.

Some learners who have recently completed their programme know this only too well.

- I really appreciated having the opportunity to take part in so many performances. It was hard work and I sometimes resented the fact that friends on other courses were off home at 4 p.m. when I had to stay back for rehearsals. In the end, though, it was a great opportunity to develop my acting and dance skills in a realistic environment.
- Looking back on my course I am really proud of myself, but I do have some regrets. I was disappointed when I didn't get the lead role in one of the major productions and then didn't put as much work into the project as I should have done. I thought I was making a point, but in the end it was only me that suffered.
- Some of the visits we went on were great. Going backstage at a professional theatre was amazing. It really gave me the impetus to work hard on my course. I remember standing on the stage of the Hippodrome thinking, "this is where I want to be some day."
- In the second year of the course I had some problems because I had to look after my little sister while my Mum was in hospital. My tutor was really great about it and helped me to negotiate extended deadlines for some of my assignments. If I was to give advice to anyone having problems that are affecting their work on their course I would tell them to speak to their tutor right away.
- Sessions with visiting tutors who actually are working in the performing arts industry were great. It gave us a fantastic opportunity to quiz them about what a career in the performing arts is really like and what we need to do to succeed.
- I found the business unit really challenging. It was about researching and presenting information and this is not my strong point. When I completed and passed the unit though it gave me a great sense of achievement.
- I just can't believe how quickly my two years has gone. We have done so much and I have really progressed as an actor. I didn't really need to use any of the support available but it was good to know it was in place if I did any have problems.

Reflection points

- What are your thoughts and feelings as you begin your course?
- What opportunities do you think being on a BTEC National will provide you with?
- Can you foresee any potential problems?

If your course takes one or two years to complete, then it is highly likely that you will experience some highs and lows in that time. You may find one or two topics harder than the rest. There may be distractions in your personal life to cope with. All of which means than you may not always be able to do your best.

It is, therefore, sensible to have an action plan to help you cope. It's also wise to plan how to make the best of opportunities for additional experiences or learning. This section shows you how to do this.

TOP TIP

Because life rarely runs smoothly, it's sensible to capitalise on the opportunities that come your way and have a plan to deal with problems.

Making the most of your opportunities

There will be many opportunities for learning on your course, not all of which will be in school or college. You should prepare for some of the following to maximise the opportunities that each offer.

- **External visits**. Prepare in advance by reading about relevant topics. Make notes when you are there. Write up your notes neatly and file them safely for future reference.
- **Visiting speakers**. Questions can usually be submitted to the speaker in advance. Think carefully about information that you would find helpful. Make notes, unless someone has been appointed to make notes for the whole group. You may be asked to thank the speaker on behalf of your group.
- **Work experience**. If work experience is an essential part of your course, your tutor will help you to organise your placement and tell you about the evidence you need to obtain. You may also get a special logbook in which to record your experiences. Read and re-read the units to which your evidence will apply and make sure you understand the grading criteria and what you need to obtain. Make time to write up your notes, logbook and/or diary every night (if possible), while everything is fresh in your mind.
- **In your own workplace**. If you have a full-time or part-time job, watch for opportunities to find out more about relevant topics that relate to your course, such as health and safety, teamwork, dealing with customers, IT security and communications. Your employer will have had to address all of these issues. Finding out more about these issues will broaden your knowledge and give more depth to your assessment responses.
- **Television, newspapers, podcasts and other information sources**. The media can be an invaluable source of information. Look out for news bulletins relating to your studies, as well as information in topical television programmes – from *The Apprentice* to *Top Gear*. You can also read news headlines online (see page 63). Podcasts are useful, too. It will help if you know what topics you will be studying in the months to come, so you can spot useful opportunities as they arise.

TOP TIP

Remember that you can use online catch-up services, such as the BBC iPlayer or 4oD (for Channel 4 shows) to see TV programmes you have missed recently.

Minimising problems

Hopefully, any problems you experience during your course will only be minor; such as struggling to find an acceptable working method with someone in your team.

You should already know who to talk to about these issues, and who to go to if that person is absent or you would prefer to talk to someone else. If your problems are affecting your work, it's sensible to see your tutor promptly. It is a rare learner who is enthusiastic about every topic and gets on well with everyone else doing the course, so your tutor won't be surprised and will give you useful guidance (in confidence) to help.

TOP TIP

Don't delay talking to someone in confidence if you have a serious problem. If your course tutor is unavailable, talk to another staff member you like and trust.

Other sources of help

If you are unfortunate enough to have a more serious personal problem, the following sources of help may be available in your centre.

- **Professional counselling.** There may be a professional counselling service. If you see a counsellor, nothing you say during the session can be mentioned to another member of staff without your permission.
- **Complaint procedures.** If you have a serious complaint, the first step is to talk to your tutor. If you can't resolve your problem informally, there will be a formal learner complaint procedure. These procedures are used only for serious issues, not for minor difficulties.
- **Appeals procedures.** If you disagree with your final grade for an assignment, check the grading criteria and ask the subject tutor to explain how the grade was awarded. If you are still unhappy, talk to your personal tutor. If you still disagree, you have the right to make a formal appeal.
- **Disciplinary procedures.** These exist for when learners consistently flout a centre's rules and ensure that all learners are dealt with in the same way. Hopefully, you will never get into trouble, but you should make sure that you read these procedures carefully to see what could happen if you did. Remember that being honest and making a swift apology is always the wisest course of action.
- **Serious illness.** Whether this involves you, a family member or a close friend, it could affect your attendance. Discuss the problem with your tutor promptly; you will be missing information from the first day you are absent. There are many solutions in this type of situation – such as sending notes by post and updating you electronically (providing you are well enough to cope with the work.)

TOP TIP

It's important to know your centre's procedures for dealing with important issues such as complaints, major illnesses, learner appeals and disciplinary matters.

Key points

- Don't miss opportunities to learn more about relevant topics through external visits, listening to visiting speakers, work experience, being at work or even watching television.
- If you have difficulties or concerns, talk to your tutor, or another appropriate person, promptly to make sure your work isn't affected.

Action points

1 Prepare in advance to maximise your opportunities.

  a) List the opportunities available on your course for obtaining more information and talking to experts. You can check with your tutor to make sure you've identified them all.

  b) Check the content of each unit you will be studying so that you know the main topics and focus of each.

  c) Identify the information that may be relevant to your course on television, on radio, in newspapers and in podcasts.

2 Make sure you know how to cope if you have a serious problem.

  a) Check your centre's procedures so you know who to talk to in a crisis, and who to contact if that person is absent.

  b) Find out where you can get hold of a copy of the main procedures in your centre that might affect you if you have a serious problem. Then read them.

Activity: Knowing where to turn

Knowing where to go if you have a problem is really important. Find out who you would go to discuss the following problems or issues.

Issue or problem	Where would you go for help?
You don't understand why you have been given a low grade for an assignment.	
The first public performance is coming up and you are really nervous and thinking of backing out.	
You are struggling with the work for a particular unit.	
You need help completing a written piece of work.	
You are having difficulty finding money for travel costs.	
You can't always stay back for rehearsals because of family or work commitments.	

TOP TIP

The time and effort you will be putting into this course deserves to be rewarded. Make sure you know how to confront and successfully overcome problems.

AND FINALLY ...

Refer to this Study Skills Guide whenever you need to remind yourself about something related to your course. Keep it in a safe place so that you can use it whenever you need to refresh your memory. That way, you'll get the very best out of your course – and yourself!

Your Study Skills Guide will help you gain the skills you need for success.

Skills building

This section has been written to help you improve the skills needed to do your best in your assignments. You may be excellent at some skills already, others may need further work. The skills you can expect to demonstrate on your course include:

- your personal, learning and thinking skills (**PLTS**)
- your **functional skills** of ICT, maths/numeracy and English
- your proofreading and document production skills.

Personal, learning and thinking skills (PLTS)

These are the skills, personal qualities and behaviour that enable you to operate more independently, work more confidently with other people and be more effective at work. You'll develop these on your BTEC Level 3 National course through a variety of experiences and as you take on different roles and responsibilities.

The skills are divided into six groups:

1. **Independent enquirers** can process and evaluate information they investigate from different perspectives. They can plan what to do and how to do it, and take into account the consequences of making different decisions.
2. **Creative thinkers** generate and explore different ideas. They make connections between ideas, events and experiences that enable them to be inventive and imaginative.
3. **Reflective learners** can assess themselves and other people. They can evaluate their own strengths and limitations. They set themselves realistic goals, monitor their own performance and welcome feedback.
4. **Team workers** collaborate with other people to achieve common goals. They are fair and considerate to others, whether as a team leader or team member, and take account of different opinions.
5. **Self-managers** are well-organised and show personal responsibility, initiative, creativity and enterprise. They look for new challenges and responsibilities and are flexible when priorities change.
6. **Effective participators** play a full part in the life of their school, college, workplace or wider community by taking responsible action to bring improvements for others as well as themselves.

Action points

1. Many parts of this Study Skills Guide relate to the development of your own personal, learning and thinking skills. For each of the following, suggest the main skill groups to which the chapter relates. Refer to the box above and write a number next to each chapter title below.

    a) Use your time wisely. ____

    b) Understand how to research and analyse information. ____

    c) Work productively as a member of a group. ____

    d) Understand yourself. ____

    e) Utilise all your resources. ____

    f) Maximise your opportunities and manage your problems. ____

2 You have been on your BTEC National course for a few months now and, although everyone is enjoying the work, you realise that some of the learners have complaints.

Firstly, several learners object to an increase in the price of printouts and photocopying, on the basis that they can't do good work for their assignments if this is too expensive. You disagree and think that the prices are reasonable, given the cost of paper.

Secondly, a timetable change means your 2 pm – 4 pm Friday afternoon class has been moved to 9 am – 11 am. Some learners are annoyed and want it changed back, while others are delighted.

a) For the first problem, identify four factors which could indicate that those complaining about the price rise might be justified.

1

2

3

4

b) For the second problem:

i) Think about which learners in your group would be most affected by the timetable change. Who might be most disturbed? Who might benefit from the earlier start?

ii) Try to think of a creative solution, or compromise, that would please both groups.

c) During the discussions about these issues, some quieter members of the class are often shouted down by the more excitable members. Suggest a strategy for dealing with this, which everyone is likely to accept.

You can also check your ideas with the suggestions given on page 85.

3 a) Complete the chart opposite, identifying occasions when you may need to demonstrate personal, learning and thinking skills in your future career. Alternatively, apply each area to a part-time job you are currently doing.

b) Identify areas where you think you are quite strong and put a tick in the 'S' column. Check that you could provide evidence to support this judgement, such as a time when you have demonstrated this skill.

c) Now consider areas where you are not so good and put a cross in the 'W' column.

d) Then practise self-management by identifying two appropriate goals to achieve over the next month and make a note of them in the space provided. If possible, talk through your ideas at your next individual tutorial.

Personal, learning and thinking skills for future career/current part-time job				
Skill group	**Example skills**	**Occasions when you use/ will use skill**	**S**	**W**
Independent enquirers	Finding information Solving problems Making decisions Reconciling conflicting information or views Justifying decisions			
Creative thinkers	Finding imaginative solutions Making original connections Finding new ways to do something Opportunities for being innovative and inventive			
Reflective learners	Goals you may set yourself Reviewing your own progress Encouraging feedback Dealing with setbacks or criticism			
Team workers	Working with others Coping with different views to your own Adapting your behaviour Being fair and considerate			
Self-managers	Being self-starting and showing initiative Dealing positively with changing priorities Organising your own time and resources Dealing with pressure Managing your emotions			
Effective participators	Identifying issues of concern to others Proposing ways forward Identifying improvements for others Influencing other people Putting forward a persuasive argument			
Goals	1			
	2			

Functional skills

Functional skills are practical skills that everyone needs to have in order to study and work effectively. They involve using and applying English, maths and ICT.

Improving your literacy skills

Your written English communication skills

A good vocabulary increases your ability to explain yourself clearly. Work that is presented without spelling and punctuation errors looks professional, and increases the likelihood of someone understanding your intended meaning. Your written communication skills will be tested in many assignments. You should work at improving areas of weakness, such as spelling, punctuation or vocabulary.

Try the following to help you improve your written communication skills:

- Read more as this introduces you to new words, and it will help your spelling.
- Look up new words in a dictionary and try to use them in conversation.
- Use a Thesaurus (you can access one electronically in Word) to find alternatives to words you use a lot, this adds variety to your work.
- Never use words you don't understand in the hope that they sound impressive.
- Write neatly, so people can read what you've written.
- Do crosswords to improve your word power and spelling.
- Improve your punctuation – especially the use of apostrophes – either by using an online programme or by using a communication textbook.
- See page 86 to gain access to some helpful websites.

Verbal and non-verbal communication (NVC) skills

Talking appropriately means using the right words and 'tone'; using the right body language means sending positive signals to reinforce this message – such as smiling at someone when you say 'Hello'. Both verbal and non-verbal communication skills are essential when dealing with people at work.

The following are some hints for successful communication:

- Be polite, tactful and sensitive to other people's feelings.
- Think about the words and phrases that you like to hear, and use them when communicating with other people.
- Use simple language so that people can understand you easily. Explain what you mean, when necessary.
- Speak at the right pace. Don't speak so slowly that everyone loses interest, or so fast that no-one can understand you.
- Speak loudly enough for people to hear you clearly – but don't shout!
- Think about the specific needs of different people – whether you are talking to a senior manager, an important client, a shy colleague or an angry customer.
- Recognise the importance of non-verbal communication (NVC) so that you send positive signals by smiling, making eye contact, giving an encouraging nod or leaning forwards to show interest.
- Read other people's body language to spot if they are anxious or impatient so that you can react appropriately.

TOP TIP

Make sure you use the right tone for the person you're talking to. Would you talk to an adult in the same way you'd talk to a very young child?

Action points

1 Go to page 86 to find out how you can gain access to websites which can help you to improve your literacy skills.

2 A battery made in China contained the following information.

DO NOT CONNECT IMPROPERLY CHARGE OR DISPOSE OF IN FIRE

a) Can you see any problems with this? Give a reason for your answer.

b) Reword the information so that it is unambiguous.

3 If you ever thought you could completely trust the spellchecker on your computer, type the text given in box A on the next page into your computer. Your spellchecker will not highlight a single error; yet even at a glance you should be able to spot dozens of errors!

Read the passage in box A and try to understand it. Then rewrite it in box B on the next page without spelling, grammatical or punctuation errors. Compare your finished work with the suggested version on page 85.

Box A

Anyone desirable to write books or reports, be they short or long, should strive too maximise they're optimal use of one's English grammar and obliviously there is an need for correct spelling two one should not neglect punctuation neither.

Frequent lea, many people and individuals become confusing or just do not no it, when righting, when words that mean different, when sounding identically, or when pronounced very similar, are knot too bee spelled inn the same whey. The quay two suck seeding is dew care, a lack off witch Leeds too Miss Spellings that mite otherwise of bean a voided. Spell chequers donut find awl missed takes.

Despite all the pitfalls how ever, with practise, patients and the right altitude, any one can soon become a grate writer and speaker, as what I did.

Box B Now rewrite the passage in the space below without errors.

4 In each of the statements listed in the table below, suggest what the body language described might mean.

Statement	What might this body language mean?
a) You are talking to your manager when he steps away from you and crosses his arms over his chest.	
b) You are talking to your friend about what she did at the weekend but she's avoiding making eye contact with you.	
c) During a tutorial session, your tutor is constantly tapping his fingers on the arm of his chair.	
d) Whenever you talk to your friend about your next assignment she bites her lower lip.	

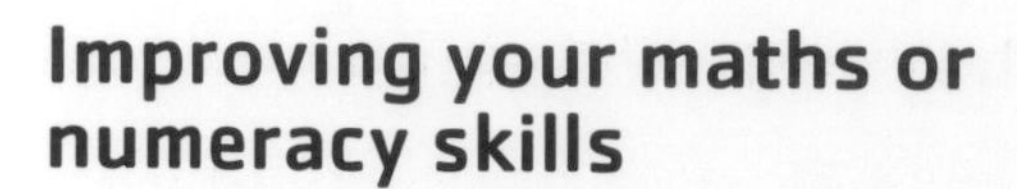

Improving your maths or numeracy skills

If you think numeracy isn't relevant to you, then think again! Numeracy is an essential life skill. If you can't carry out basic calculations accurately then you will have problems, perhaps when you least expect them. You'll often encounter numbers in various contexts – sometimes they will be correctly given, sometimes not. Unless you have a basic understanding about numeracy, you won't be able to tell the difference.

Good numeracy skills will improve your ability to express yourself, especially in assignments and at work. If you have problems, there are strategies that you can practise to help:

- Do basic calculations in your head, then check them on a calculator.
- Ask your tutor for help if important calculations give you problems.
- When you are using your computer, use the onscreen calculator (or a spreadsheet package) to do calculations.
- Investigate puzzle sites and brain training software, such as Dr Kageyama's Maths Training by Nintendo.

Action points

1 Go to page 86 to find out how you can gain access to websites which can help you to improve your numeracy skills.

2 Try the following task with a friend or family member.

Each of you should write down 36 simple calculations in a list, e.g. 8 × 6, 19 – 8, 14 + 6. Exchange lists. See who can answer the most calculations correctly in the shortest time.

3 Figures aren't always what they appear to be. For example, Sophie watches *Who Wants To Be A Millionaire?* She hears Chris Tarrant say that there have been over 500 shows, with 1200 contestants who have each won over £50,000 on average. Five people have won £1 million.

Sophie says she is going to enter because she is almost certain to win more than £50,000 and could even win a million pounds.

a) On the figures given, what is the approximate total of money won over 500 shows (to the nearest £ million)?

b) Assuming that Sophie is chosen to appear on the show, and makes it on air as a contestant, do you think Sophie's argument that she will 'almost certainly' win more than £50,000 is correct? Give a reason for your answer. (The correct answer is on page 86.)

4 You have a part-time job and have been asked to carry out a survey on the usage of the drinks vending machine. Of the 500 people surveyed:

- 225 use the machine to buy one cup of coffee only
- 100 use the machine to buy one cup of tea only
- 75 use the machine to buy one cup of cold drinks only
- 50 use the machine to buy one cup of hot chocolate only
- the rest are non-users
- the ratio of male to female users is 2:1.

a) How many men in your survey use the machine?

b) How many women in your survey use the machine?

c) Calculate the proportion of the people in your survey that use the machine. Express this as a fraction and a percentage.

d) What is the ratio of coffee drinkers to tea drinkers in your survey?

e) What is the ratio of coffee drinkers to hot chocolate drinkers in your survey?

f) If people continue to purchase from the machine in the same ratio found in your survey, and last month 1800 cups of coffee were sold, what would you expect the sales of the cold drinks to be?

g) Using the answer to f), if coffee costs 65p and all cold drinks cost 60p, how much would have been spent in total last month on these two items?

Improving your ICT skills

Good ICT skills are an asset in many aspects of your daily life and not just for those studying to be IT practitioners.

The following are ways in which you can Improve your ICT skills:

- Check that you can use the main features of the software packages you need to produce your assignments, eg Word, Excel and PowerPoint.
- Choose a good search engine and learn to use it properly. Go to page 86 to find out how you can access a useful website.
- Developing and using your IT skills enables you to enhance your assignments. This may include learning how to import and export text and artwork from one package to another; taking digital photographs and inserting them into your work and/or creating drawings or diagrams by using appropriate software.

Action points

1 Check your basic knowledge of IT terminology by identifying each of these items on your computer screen:

a) taskbar
b) toolbar
c) title bar
d) menu bar
e) mouse pointer
f) scroll bars
g) status bar
h) insertion point
i) maximise/minimise button.

2 Assess your IT skills by identifying the packages and operations you find easy to use and those that you find more difficult. If you use Microsoft Office products (Word, PowerPoint, Access or Excel) you can find out more about improving your skills online. Go to page 86 to find out how you can access a website to help you with this task.

3 Search the internet to find a useful dictionary of IT terms. Bookmark it for future use. Find out the meaning of any of the following terms that you don't know already:
 a) portal
 b) cached link
 c) home page
 d) browser
 e) firewall
 f) HTML
 g) URL
 h) cookie
 i) hyperlink
 j) freeware.

Proofreading and document preparation skills

Improving your keyboard, document production and general IT skills can save you hours of time. When you have good skills, the work you produce will be of a far more professional standard.

- Think about learning to touch type. Your centre may have a workshop you can join, or you can use an online program – go to page 86 to find out how you can access a useful website. From here you can access websites that will allow you to test and work on improving your typing skills.
- Obtain correct examples of any document formats you will have to use, such as a report or summary, either from your tutor, the internet or from a textbook.
- Proofread all your work carefully. A spellchecker won't find all your mistakes, so you must read through it yourself as well.
- Make sure your work looks professional by using a suitable typeface and font size, as well as reasonable margins.
- Print your work and store the printouts neatly, so that it stays in perfect condition for when you hand it in.

Action points

1 You can check and improve your typing skills using online typing sites – see link in previous section.

2 Check your ability to create documents by scoring yourself out of 5 for each of the following questions, where 5 is something you can do easily and 0 is something you can't do at all. Then focus on improving every score where you rated yourself 3 or less.

 I know how to:
 a) create a new document and open a saved document _____
 b) use the mouse to click, double-click and drag objects _____
 c) use drop-down menus _____
 d) customise my toolbars by adding or deleting options _____
 e) save and/or print a document _____
 f) create folders and sub-folders to organise my work _____
 g) move a folder I use regularly to My Places _____
 h) amend text in a document _____
 i) select, copy, paste and delete information in a document _____
 j) quickly find and replace text in a document _____
 k) insert special characters _____
 l) create a table or insert a diagram in a document _____
 m) change the text size, font and colour _____
 n) add bold, italics or underscore _____
 o) create a bullet or numbered list _____
 p) align text left, right or centred _____
 q) format pages before they are printed _____
 r) proofread a document so that there are no mistakes _____.

Answers

Activity: Let's give you a tip... (page 62)

a) i) Fact
ii) Opinion – the number cannot be validated
iii) Fact
iv) Opinion
v) Opinion
vi) Opinion – again the number is estimated

Skills building answers

PLTS Action points (page 75)

1 a) Use your time wisely = **5** Self-managers
b) Understand how to research and analyse information = **1** Independent enquirers, **5** Self-managers
c) Work productively as a member of a group = **4** Team workers, **6** Effective participators
d) Understand yourself = **3** Reflective learners
e) Utilise all your resources = **5** Self-managers
f) Maximise your opportunities and manage your problems = **1** Independent enquirers, **2** Creative thinkers, **3** Reflective learners, **5** Self-managers

2 a) Factors to consider in relation to the increased photocopying/printing charges include: the comparative prices charged by other schools/colleges, how often there is a price rise, whether any printing or photocopying at all can be done without charge, whether there are any concessions for special tasks or assignments, the availability of class sets of books/popular library books for loan (which reduces the need for photocopying.)

b) i) An earlier start will be more likely to negatively affect those who live further away and who are reliant on public transport, particularly in rural areas. The earlier finish will benefit anyone who has a part-time job that starts on a Friday afternoon or who has after college commitments, such as looking after younger sisters or brothers.
ii) The scope for compromise would depend on whether there are any classes between 11 am and 2 pm on a Friday, whether tutors had any flexibility and whether the new 9 am – 11 am class could be moved to another time or day.

c) One strategy would be to allow discussion for a set time, ensure everyone had spoken, then put the issue to a vote. The leader should prompt suggestions from quieter members by asking people individually what they think.

Literacy skills action points (page 79)

2 a) The statement reads as if it is acceptable to either charge it or dispose of it in fire.
b) Do not connect this battery improperly. Do not recharge it and do not dispose of it in fire.

3 Anyone who wishes to write books or reports, whether short or long, should try to use English grammatically. Obviously there is a need for correct spelling, too. Punctuation should also not be neglected.

Frequently, people confuse words with different meanings when they are writing, especially when these sound identical or very similar, even when they must not be spelled in the same way. The key to succeeding is due care, a lack of which leads to misspellings that might otherwise have been avoided. Spellcheckers do not find all mistakes.

Despite all the pitfalls, however, with practice, patience and the right attitude, anyone can soon become a great writer and speaker, like me.

4 Possible answers

a) Stepping backwards and crossing arms across the chest might indicate that your manager is creating a barrier between you and himself, or that he is angry.

b) Your friend might be feeling guilty about what she did at the weekend or not confident that you will approve of what she tells you.

c) Your tutor might be frustrated as he has many things to do and so wants the tutorial to be over quickly.

d) Your friend might be anxious about the next assignment or about the time she has to complete it.

Numeracy action points (page 82)

3 a) £60 million

b) Sophie's argument is incorrect as £50,000 is an average, i.e. some contestants will win more, but many will win much less. The distribution of prizes is greater at lower amounts because more people win small amounts of money than large amounts – and only five have won the top prize of £1 million.

4 a) 300

b) 150

c) 9/10ths, 90%

d) 225:100 (= 45:20) = 9:4

e) 225:50 = 9:2

f) 600

g) £1530

Accessing website links

Links to various websites are referred to throughout this BTEC Level 3 National Study Skills Guide. To ensure that these links are up-to-date, that they work and that the sites aren't inadvertently linked to any material that could be considered offensive, we have made the links available on our website: www.pearsonhotlinks.co.uk. When you visit the site, search for either the title BTEC Level 3 National Study Skills Guide in Performing Arts or ISBN 9781846905667. From here you can gain access to the website links and information on how they can be used to help you with your studies.

Useful terms

Accreditation of Prior Learning (APL)
Some of your previous achievements and experiences may be able to be used to count towards your qualification.

Apprenticeships
Schemes that enable you to work and earn money at the same time as you gain further qualifications (an NVQ award and a technical certificate) and improve your functional skills. Apprentices learn work-based skills relevant to their job role and their chosen industry. See page 86 for information on accessing a website to find out more.

Assessment methods
Techniques used to check that your work demonstrates the learning and understanding required for your qualification, such as assignments, case studies and practical tasks.

Assessor
An assessor is the tutor who marks or assesses your work.

Assignment
A complex task or mini-project set to meet specific grading criteria and learning outcomes.

Awarding body
An organisation responsible for devising, assessing and issuing qualifications. The awarding body for all BTEC qualifications is Edexcel.

Credit value
The number of credits attached to your BTEC course. The credit value increases in relation to the length of time you need to complete the course, from 30 credits for a BTEC Level 3 Certificate, 60 credits for a Subsidiary Diploma, 120 credits for a Diploma, up to 180 credits for an Extended Diploma.

Degrees
Higher education qualifications offered by universities and colleges. Foundation degrees take two years to complete; honours degrees may take three years or longer.

Department for Business Innovation and Skills (BIS)
BIS is responsible for further and higher education and skills training, as well as functions related to trade and industry. See page 86 for information on accessing a website to find out more.

Department for Education
The Department for Education is the government department responsible for schools and education, as well as for children's services. See page 86 for information on accessing a website to find out more.

Distance learning
When you learn and/or study for a qualification at home or at work. You communicate with your tutor and/or the centre that organises the course by post, telephone or electronically.

Educational Maintenance Award (EMA)
An EMA is a means-tested award that provides eligible learners under 19, who are studying a full-time course at school or college, with a cash sum of money every week. See page 86 for information on accessing a website to find out more.

External verification
Formal checking of the programme by an Edexcel representative that focuses on sampling various assignments to check content, accurate assessment and grading.

Forbidden combinations
There are some qualifications that cannot be taken simultaneously because their content is too similar.

Functional skills
Practical skills in English, maths and ICT that enable people to work confidently, effectively and independently. Level 2 Functional Skills are mapped to the units of BTEC Level 3 National qualifications. They aren't compulsory to achieve on the course, but are of great use.

Grade boundaries
Pre-set points that determine whether you will achieve a pass, merit or distinction as the overall final grade(s) for your qualification.

Grading criteria
The specific evidence you have to demonstrate to obtain a particular grade in the unit.

Grading domains
The main areas of learning that support the learning outcomes. On a BTEC Level 3 National course these are: application of knowledge and understanding; development of practical and technical skills; personal development for occupational roles; application of PLTS and functional skills.

Grading grid
The table in each unit of your qualification specification that sets out what you have to show you can do.

Higher education (HE)
Post-secondary and post-further education, usually provided by universities and colleges.

Higher-level skills
These are skills such as evaluating or critically assessing information. They are more difficult than lower-level skills such as writing a description or making a list. You must be able to demonstrate higher-level skills to achieve a distinction.

Indicative reading
Recommended books and journals whose content is both suitable and relevant for the BTEC unit studied.

Induction
A short programme of events at the start of a course designed to give you essential information, and introduce you to your fellow learners and tutors, so that you can settle down as quickly and easily as possible.

Internal verification
The quality checks carried out by nominated tutors at your school or college to ensure that all assignments are at the right level, cover appropriate learning outcomes and grading criteria, and that all assessors are marking work consistently and to the same standard.

Investors in People (IiP)
A national quality standard that sets a level of good practice for training and developing of people within a business. Participating organisations must demonstrate commitment to achieve the standard.

Learning outcomes
The knowledge and skills you must demonstrate to show that you have effectively learned a unit.

Learning support
Additional help that is available to all learners in a school or college who have learning difficulties or other special needs.

Levels of study
The depth, breadth and complexity of knowledge, understanding and skills required to achieve a qualification, which also determines its level. Level 2 equates to GCSE level and Level 3 equates to A-level. As you successfully achieve one level, you can then progress to the next. BTEC qualifications are offered at Entry Level, then Levels 1, 2, 3, 4 and 5.

Local Education Authority (LEA)
The local government body responsible for providing education for all learners of compulsory school age. The LEA is also responsible for managing the education budget for 16–19 learners in its area.

Mandatory units
These are units that all learners must complete to gain a qualification; in this case a BTEC Level 3 National. Some BTEC qualifications have an over-arching title, eg Construction, but within Construction you can choose different pathways. Your chosen pathway may have additional mandatory units specific to that pathway.

Mentor
A more experienced person who will guide you and counsel you if you have a problem or difficulty.

Mode of delivery
The way in which a qualification is offered to learners for example, part-time, full-time, as a short course or by distance learning.

National Occupational Standard (NOS)
Statements of the skills, knowledge and understanding you need to develop in order to be competent at a particular job.

National Vocational Qualification (NVQ)
Qualifications that concentrate on the practical skills and knowledge required to do a job competently. They are usually assessed in the workplace and range from Level 1 (the lowest) to Level 5 (the highest).

Nested qualifications
Qualifications that have 'common' units, so that learners can easily progress from one to another by adding on more units

Ofqual
The public body responsible for regulating qualifications, exams and tests in England.

Optional units
Units on your course from which you may be able to make a choice. They help you specialise your skills, knowledge and understanding and may help progression into work or further education.

Pathway
All BTEC Level 3 National qualifications comprise a small number of mandatory units and a larger number of optional units. These units are grouped into different combinations to provide alternative pathways to achieving the qualification. These pathways are usually linked to different career preferences.

Peer review
This involves feedback on your performance by your peers (members of your team, or class group.) You will also be given an opportunity to review their performance.

Plagiarism
The practice of copying someone else's work, or work from any other sources (eg the internet), and passing it off as your own. This practice is strictly forbidden on all courses.

Personal, learning and thinking skills (PLTS)
The skills, personal qualities and behaviour that improve your ability to work independently. Developing these skills makes you more effective and confident at work. Opportunities for developing these skills are a feature of all BTEC Level 3 National courses. These skills aren't compulsory to achieve on the course, but are of great use to you.

Portfolio
A collection of work compiled by a learner, usually as evidence of learning, to present to an assessor.

Procrastinator
Someone who is forever putting off or delaying work, either because they are lazy or because they have poor organisational skills.

Professional body
An organisation that exists to promote or support a particular profession; for example, the Royal Institute of British Architects (RIBA).

Professional development and training
This involves undertaking activities relevant to your job to increase and/or update your knowledge and skills.

Project
A project is a comprehensive piece of work, which normally involves original research and investigation by an individual or by a team. The findings and results may be presented in writing and summarised as a presentation.

Qualifications and Credit Framework (QCF)
The QCF is a framework for recognising skills and qualifications. It does this by awarding credit for qualifications and units so that they are easier to measure and compare. All BTEC Level 3 National qualifications are part of the QCF.

Qualifications and Curriculum Development Agency (QCDA)
The QCDA is responsible for maintaining and developing the national curriculum, delivering assessments, tests and examinations and reforming qualifications.

Quality assurance
In education, this is the process of continually checking that a course of study is meeting the specific requirements set down by the awarding body.

Sector Skills Councils (SSCs)
The 25 employer-led, independent organisations responsible for improving workforce skills in the UK by identifying skill gaps and improving learning in the workplace. Each council covers a different type of industry.

Semester
Many universities and colleges divide their academic year into two halves or semesters, one from September to January and one from February to July.

Seminar
A learning event involving a group of learners and a tutor, which may be learner-led, and follow research into a topic that has been introduced at an earlier stage.

Study buddy
A person in your group or class who takes notes for you and keeps you informed of important developments if you are absent. You do the same for them in return.

Time-constrained assignment
An assessment you must complete within a fixed time limit.

Tutorial
An individual or small group meeting with your tutor at which you can discuss your current work and other more general course issues. At an individual tutorial, your progress on the course will be discussed and you can raise any concerns or personal worries you may have.

The University and Colleges Admissions Service (UCAS)
UCAS (pronounced 'you-cass') is the central organisation that processes all applications for higher education (HE) courses.

UCAS points
The number of points allocated by UCAS for the qualifications you have obtained. Higher education institutions specify how many points you need to be accepted on the courses they offer. See page 86 for information on accessing a website to find out more.

Unit abstract
The summary at the start of each BTEC unit that tells you what the unit is about.

Unit content
Details about the topics covered by the unit and the knowledge and skills you need to complete it.

Unit points
The number of points you gain when you complete a unit. These will depend on the grade you achieve (pass, merit or distinction).

Vocational qualification
Designed to develop knowledge and understanding relevant to a chosen area of work.

Work experience
Time you spend on an employer's premises when you learn about the enterprise, carry out work-based tasks and develop skills and knowledge.

Please note that all information given within these useful terms was correct at the time of going to print.